Untangling Anxiety:
A Guide to Reclaiming Control and Confidence

Piper Harris, MA, NPT-C

For permission requests, contact:
Piper Harris
Untangled Mind, LLC
info@untangledmind.net

ISBN:979-8-9927856-1-6
First Edition – April 2025

Welcome to Your Journey of Overcoming Anxiety

Building a Foundation for Lasting Change

Healing isn't a one-time event; it's a structured process. Think of it like constructing a bridge—without a solid foundation, it won't hold up under the weight of life's challenges. The framework in this workbook is designed to provide stability, guiding you step by step toward growth and resilience.

To effectively manage anxiety, we must first lay the groundwork before diving into deeper exploration. Each stage builds upon the last, ensuring a strong and sustainable approach to healing.

- **Establishing Stability** – The journey begins by creating a sense of emotional and psychological security within yourself and your environment.
- **Recognizing Core Needs** – Identifying and addressing both physical and emotional needs forms a crucial foundation for progress.
- **Gaining Knowledge** – Understanding how anxiety affects your thoughts, emotions, and behaviors allows you to engage in meaningful change.
- **Developing Regulation Skills** – Learning to manage intense emotions and calm your nervous system is a key part of navigating anxiety effectively.
- **Unpacking Patterns** – Recognizing how past experiences shape your responses empowers you to break unhelpful cycles.
- **Applying CBT Strategies** – With a solid base in place, you can begin reshaping thought patterns, challenging anxious beliefs, and using evidence-based tools for lasting relief.
- **Living with Intention** – Finally, you'll integrate these skills to build resilience and pursue a life rooted in confidence and purpose.

This workbook follows that same structure. You will begin by addressing core needs and understanding how anxiety functions, then gradually move into techniques for reframing negative thought patterns and managing overwhelming emotions.

By the end, you will have a comprehensive toolkit to help you regain control over your anxiety, deepen your self-awareness, and cultivate a more empowered approach to life. Overcoming anxiety isn't something you have to navigate alone—this workbook serves as a structured, research-backed guide to help you untangle anxious thoughts and build lasting change.

At Untangled Mind, we believe that healing should be anchored in more than just emotions or assumptions. While emotional awareness plays a vital role, true progress requires a measurable, data-driven approach.

Throughout this workbook—and in our work together—you will complete multiple assessments designed to help us track your growth and refine our approach (refer to the Assessment Tracker in the Tools and Resources section). These assessments are not about labeling or diagnosing you; instead, they serve as valuable tools to provide deeper insight into your thought patterns, behaviors, and progress over time.

By using these structured evaluations, we ensure that your journey is not dictated by fleeting emotions or subjective impressions, but by clear, actionable data. This process holds us both accountable—helping me tailor the most effective, personalized plan for you while empowering you to better understand your own patterns and areas for growth.

The goal is not to confine you with labels but to equip you with practical strategies and a clear roadmap toward lasting change.

Your Treatment Plan: A Dynamic Roadmap to Growth

Your treatment plan is a key component of your healing journey. Rather than being a static document, it is a flexible and evolving tool designed to adapt as you progress. This plan serves as a structured guide, breaking down your recovery into behavioral patterns, long-term goals, and short-term, achievable steps—all of which are designed to be measurable and manageable.

As you move forward, your treatment plan will shift and grow alongside you. Your goals and objectives are not set in stone; they are meant to be adaptable, giving you the space to refine your path as needed. That's why it's important to revisit and reflect on your treatment plan regularly—to assess where you are, acknowledge progress, and determine the next steps in your journey.

If you find that certain goals need to be adjusted, expanded, or refined, always consult your therapist. They can help you assess your progress and make any necessary modifications to ensure your plan continues to align with your evolving needs.

To stay engaged with your growth, keep your treatment plan easily accessible—whether by inserting it into this workbook or bringing it to sessions. Having it on hand allows you to track progress, stay focused on your goals, and take an active role in your healing process.

What Makes This Workbook Unique

This workbook is designed to go beyond traditional self-help resources by integrating Cognitive Behavioral Therapy (CBT), neuropsychotherapy principles, and evidence-based strategies—all presented in a practical way. While CBT serves as the foundation, what truly sets this workbook apart is its ability to bridge personal experience with actionable techniques for managing anxiety and reclaiming control over your life.

Each section is carefully structured to help you:

- Understand the root causes of your anxiety and how it has shaped your thoughts, emotions, and behaviors.
- Build awareness of your emotional and physical responses to stress and triggers.
- Develop skills to face and manage life's challenges with greater confidence and clarity.
- Stay accountable to your therapeutic goals through structured exercises, guided reflections, and practical assignments.

This workbook is more than just a collection of techniques—it is a structured yet adaptable tool designed to support you throughout your healing journey. Whether used independently or alongside therapy, it serves as a companion in your growth, providing the guidance and reinforcement needed to create meaningful and lasting change.

Helpful Hints:

Purchase Stick-On Tabs for Easy Access

To make navigating this workbook even easier, consider purchasing stick-on tabs that you can place on the sides of the pages. These tabs will allow you to quickly access specific sections without having to flip through the entire workbook. Whether it's your treatment plan, assessment results, or any of the exercises you'll return to often, tabs will help keep you organized and efficient.

By adding tabs to key sections, you'll be able to easily refer to the most important parts of your journey without losing momentum. This small investment in organization can make a big difference in helping you stay on track with your goals. Plus, it's a simple tool to keep your progress clear and accessible!

Take Your Time with Assignments

It's important to take your time with each assignment—don't rush through them just to finish (you won't get much out of it if you complete them right before session). Healing is a process that requires attention, reflection, and effort. Give yourself the space to fully engage with the exercises and let your thoughts and feelings unfold at their own pace.

If you try to speed through, you might miss out on valuable insights. Plan ahead so that you can complete each section thoughtfully, and use your therapy sessions to discuss any challenges or breakthroughs that arise.

Set a Consistent Time for Your Routine

Creating a regular routine can make a huge difference in maintaining consistency with your healing process. Try setting aside a specific time each day to complete workbook assignments or engage in your self-reflection exercises.

This helps you build the habit of self-care and makes it easier to stay on track with your goals. Whether it's first thing in the morning or right before bed, find a time that works best for you and stick to it as much as possible.

Create a Comfortable Environment for Reflection

Set yourself up for success by creating a space where you feel comfortable and relaxed when completing your workbook assignments. Whether it's a quiet corner of your home, a cozy chair, or a coffee shop, choose a place where you can focus without distractions. Having a designated space for reflection can help you get into the right mindset for the work you're doing.

Use the "Pause and Reflect" Approach

During assignments or exercises, don't feel like you have to rush through every thought or feeling. If you come across a point that feels difficult or emotional, it's okay to pause and reflect on it for a moment. Jot down your initial thoughts or feelings, and revisit them later if needed. Healing doesn't happen in a straight line, and some moments require a little more time to process than others. Be patient with yourself and recognize when you need to take a step back.

Celebrate Small Wins

Healing can sometimes feel slow, but remember that every small step counts. Take time to celebrate your progress, no matter how minor it may seem. Whether it's finishing a section, realizing a new insight, or noticing a small shift in your emotions, these wins are important. Recognizing them can keep you motivated and remind you of the hard work you're putting into your recovery. You will find a Progress Tracker in your Tools and Ressources section of this workbook.

Step into Honesty with Your Therapist

Honesty with your therapist is one of the most important elements of your healing journey. While it may feel difficult at times, being open about your thoughts, feelings, and experiences helps create a foundation of trust and authenticity. Your therapist is there to support you, not to judge you. The more honestly you engage, the more effective your therapy will be.

Healing requires a deep level of self-awareness, and sometimes that means confronting things that are uncomfortable or even difficult to acknowledge. Whether it's your fears, insecurities, or patterns you're trying to break, sharing them openly can help you move past them. Remember, therapy is a safe space where you can express yourself freely and without fear of judgment. By stepping into honesty, you give yourself the opportunity to truly grow, address what's holding you back, and create real change.

Your Next Steps

Healing from anxiety isn't about eliminating every worry or fear—it's about reshaping how you respond to them, integrating the lessons they bring, and reclaiming control over your life. True growth comes from embracing both the struggles and the victories along the way. As you progress through this workbook, each section will build upon the last, equipping you with practical strategies to regulate emotions, challenge anxious thoughts, and reframe your experiences. With every step, you will cultivate greater clarity, emotional resilience, and a renewed sense of confidence.

This workbook is your guide, but your healing journey is uniquely yours. The effort you invest in this process—combined with the support of your therapist—lays the foundation for lasting transformation. Healing isn't a race; it unfolds in its own time, and moving at a pace that feels right for you is essential.

This is your pathway to healing, and your therapists are here to walk alongside you—helping you navigate challenges, celebrating your progress, and empowering you to build a life rooted in strength, purpose, and connection.

Therapeutic Approach

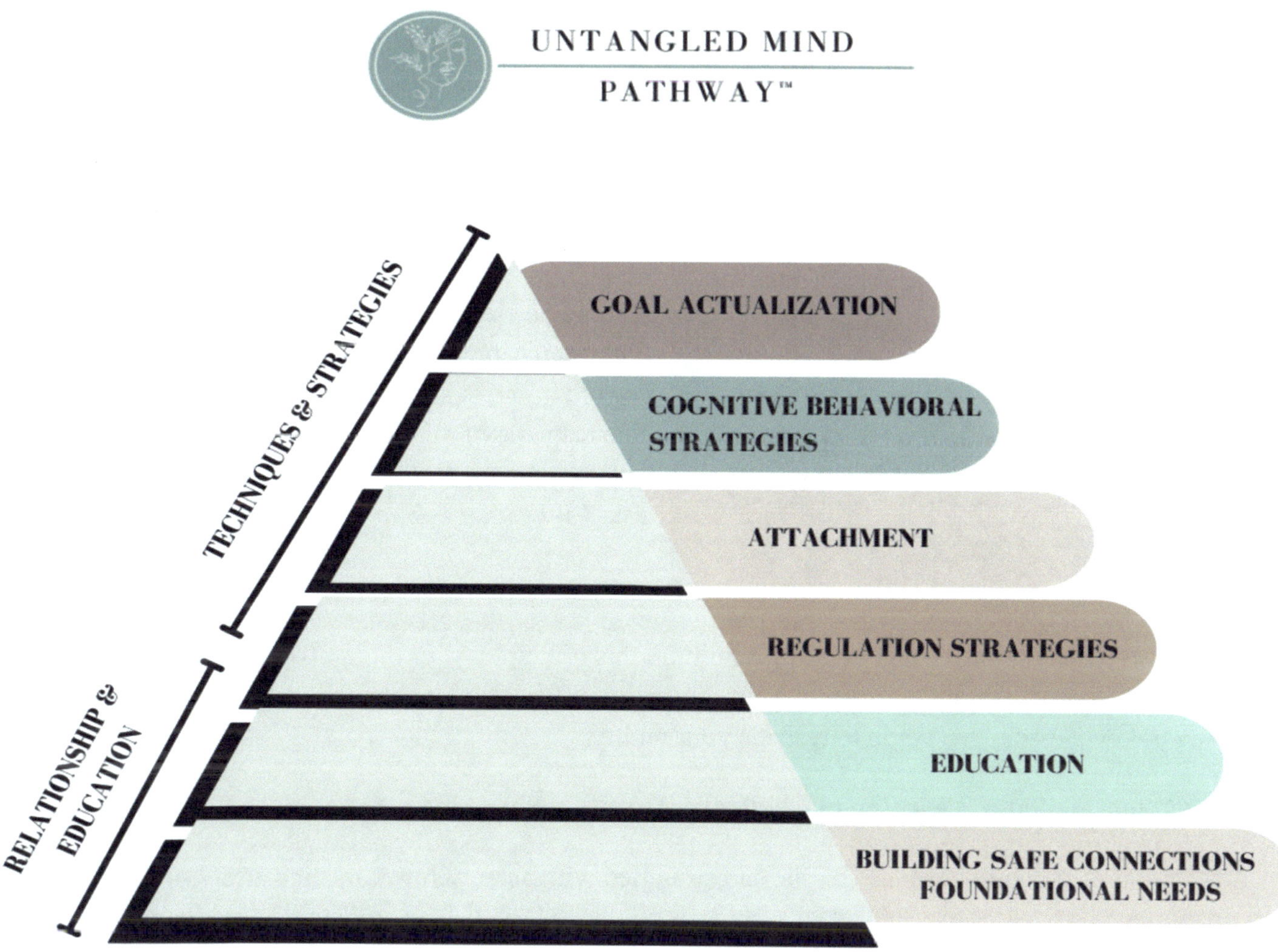

Author's Note

If you see yourself as broken, that is exactly how you will feel. That may sound blunt, but it's a truth worth confronting.

In today's world, it's easy to frame normal human experiences as disorders, turning temporary struggles into lifelong identities. While emotional distress is real, not every challenge needs a diagnosis, and not every hardship defines who you are. Yet, the mental health industry—while well-intentioned—has oftentimes reinforced the idea that a label is the only way to validate what you're going through.

Let me be clear: **labels can keep you stuck**. They can cement a rigid mindset, keeping you locked in the belief that you are "broken" rather than capable of change. Instead of asking, *"What's wrong with me?"* I encourage you to ask, *"What can I do to grow through this?"*

Cognitive Behavioral Therapy (CBT) is built on this principle: your thoughts influence your emotions, behaviors, and ultimately, your outcomes. When you learn to challenge the thoughts that hold you back, you begin to reshape your reality.

The Story of Anna: Learning to Challenge Anxiety's Narrative

Anna came to therapy exhausted. She had struggled with anxiety for years, and after experiencing a series of panic attacks, she was convinced she had an anxiety disorder that would never improve. "This is just how I am," she told me. "I've always been anxious. I'll never be able to change."

Like many people, Anna believed that her struggles defined her. Her anxious thoughts fueled avoidance, and avoidance reinforced the belief that she was powerless against her anxiety.

But as we worked together, she started to see things differently. Instead of assuming every anxious thought was a sign of disorder, we examined them as learned patterns—responses her brain had developed over time. Anxiety wasn't a personal flaw; it was a reaction, something that could be understood and changed.

Through structured CBT techniques, Anna learned to challenge her catastrophic thinking, interrupt her avoidance cycles, and gradually expose herself to the situations she feared. Over time, she recognized something powerful: she wasn't broken—she had just been stuck in a pattern that she now had the ability to change.

This workbook is designed to help you do the same. It's *not* here to reinforce the idea that anxiety controls you. Instead, it's a guide to help you question the thoughts that keep you feeling stuck and replace them with beliefs that move you forward. You are not here to be labeled—you are here to *take back control of your life.*

A Foundation Beyond CBT

While CBT is an incredibly effective tool, I would be remiss if I didn't acknowledge another cornerstone of my belief in resilience: my faith in Jesus Christ.

I recognize that not everyone shares this belief. I cannot separate the healing journey for myself and those of others, from the strength found in a relationship with Christ. Research consistently shows that faith—specifically, faith in Jesus—contributes to greater psychological resilience, stronger coping mechanisms, and a deeper sense of peace.

If faith is not a part of your life, I encourage you to still engage fully with the tools in this workbook. But I also invite you to consider: *What if healing is about more than just techniques? What if hope, faith, and purpose are just as important as the strategies we use?*

Your Healing, Your Choice

Healing is not a one-size-fits-all process. It requires patience, persistence, and a willingness to challenge what you've always believed about yourself. The strategies in this workbook are not here to fix you—because you are not broken. Instead, they will help you untangle the thoughts and behaviors that keep you stuck, equipping you with the confidence to move forward.

You've already taken the first step by opening this workbook. Now, I encourage you to take the next one: **believe in your capacity for change.**

Here's to untangling together,

Piper Harris, APC, NPT-C
Untangled Mind, LLC

Disclaimer

This workbook is a complimentary resource for self-reflection and personal growth within therapy at Untangled Mind, LLC. It is not a substitute for professional therapy or a structured therapeutic relationship.

If you are using this workbook outside of therapy with Piper Harris, please be aware that some exercises and references are meant to be explored with professional guidance. Certain concepts—particularly those related to safety, attunement, and therapeutic alliance—are best understood and applied in a working relationship with a anxiety-informed therapist.

While the tools and strategies provided can be beneficial, they are intended for informational purposes only and should not replace individualized care or crisis intervention. If you are experiencing significant distress, anxiety symptoms, or mental health challenges, please seek the guidance of a licensed mental health professional.

If you are in crisis, please reach out for immediate support. Contact a local emergency service, a crisis center, or the 988 Suicide & Crisis Lifeline.

Disclosure Statement

This workbook was developed through a combination of professional expertise and AI-assisted tools to enhance clarity and structure. AI support was used to refine the articulation of my therapeutic approach and to ensure readability through grammar and style adjustments. All concepts, exercises, and insights remain grounded in evidence-based psychological principles of my clinical experience.

LEVEL 1

Building Safe Connections & Foundational Needs

Laying the Foundation –
Safety, Stability, and Connection

Level 1: Building Safe Connections & Foundational Needs

Healing from anxiety begins with creating a sense of safety—not just in your environment, but in your relationships and within yourself. Before diving into deeper anxiety work, it's essential to establish a foundation of stability and trust. This first level of therapy focuses on two core areas:

- **Building Safe Connections** – Developing a strong therapeutic relationship where you feel supported and secure in the work we are doing together.
- **Addressing Foundational Needs** – Identifying and managing basic physical and psychological factors that may be contributing to heightened anxiety.

These are not just preliminary steps but the essential framework for meaningful progress. Without them, anxiety work can feel overwhelming, frustrating, or even counterproductive.

Building Safe Connections: The Therapeutic Alliance

Many individuals struggling with anxiety also struggle with trust—whether in relationships, institutions, or even within themselves. If your anxiety was shaped by difficult experiences with others—such as betrayal, neglect, or emotional invalidation—then relationships may feel unsafe. If your anxiety is rooted in perfectionism, over-responsibility, or chronic self-doubt, it may feel difficult to relax—even in situations that others would consider safe or familiar. The mind remains on high alert, driven by 'what ifs,' imagined outcomes, and an ongoing pressure to prevent failure or loss of control.

Therapy provides an opportunity to redefine what safe connection looks like, but this process takes time. Our work together is grounded in the understanding that healing happens when trust is built first. We will always move at a pace that feels manageable for you—whether that means gradually taking steps forward or allowing space for hesitation.

The relationship between therapist and client is one of the most significant predictors of success in therapy. Feeling heard, validated, and understood creates the security needed for meaningful change. If you do not feel comfortable in this space, progress will be limited. Trust is not assumed—it is developed over time. Through consistency, honesty, and collaborative work, we will establish a therapeutic alliance that supports your growth.

The Science Behind Connection: Mirror Neurons

Human beings are wired for connection, and neuroscience provides clear evidence of this through mirror neurons—specialized brain cells that activate both when we perform an action and when we observe someone else doing it. In other words, our brains are wired to pick up on and mirror the emotional and behavioral cues of those around us.

For individuals struggling with anxiety, this mirroring effect can reinforce self-doubt or fear of negative evaluation. Many anxious individuals are highly attuned to subtle shifts in tone, expression, or feedback, often interpreting them as signs of disapproval or rejection. These interpretations may not be accurate but are driven by a learned pattern of overanalyzing how others perceive them. In the therapeutic relationship, this can show up as hesitation to share openly, fear of being judged, or the belief that they need to present themselves a certain way to be accepted.

However, the brain is adaptable. Through new, safe, and consistent interactions, the mind can begin to recognize healthier relational patterns, gradually rewiring itself toward trust, emotional regulation, and stability. This is why establishing secure connections—whether in therapy or in everyday life—is a fundamental step in reducing anxiety and fostering long-term emotional well-being.

Attunement: More Than a Buzzword

Attunement is a core skill in anxiety recovery because it strengthens your ability to recognize what you're feeling—and why—without immediately reacting to it. Anxiety often drives reactive patterns like overthinking, avoidance, or compulsive action, all aimed at reducing uncertainty or discomfort.

When you become more attuned to your emotions, thoughts, and bodily signals, you can begin to respond to anxiety with curiosity instead of fear. This shift allows you to interrupt automatic responses, notice the early signs of escalation, and choose how you want to move forward.

Attunement is not about analyzing every feeling; it's about building self-awareness without judgment. As you improve this skill, you'll gain clarity in anxious moments, increase emotional flexibility, and develop a stronger sense of self-trust—key ingredients in building long-term resilience and confidence.

Attunement Takes Time

Attunement isn't a vague or abstract concept—it's a foundational skill in anxiety recovery. At its core, attunement is the ability to be fully present, aware, and responsive—not just to others, but to yourself. It involves recognizing subtle internal cues like physical sensations, emotional shifts, and thought patterns, and learning how to interpret them accurately rather than reactively.

For individuals struggling with anxiety, past experiences may have taught you to dismiss, suppress, or catastrophize your internal signals. If emotions were minimized or invalidated, or if you were praised only for high achievement or being "easy," you may have learned to ignore your needs and over-monitor your performance. You may now find it difficult to tell the difference between real danger and everyday discomfort—your brain may treat both the same.

Therapy gives you space to begin relearning what it means to be seen, heard, and responded to—without judgment. As your therapist, I will model attunement with you. We'll also work together to help you attune to yourself, developing the skill to notice what you're feeling and needing without jumping to conclusions or trying to "fix" it immediately.

Many anxious individuals tend to hyper-focus on physical or emotional sensations, often interpreting them as signs that something is wrong. Attunement helps you build the capacity to notice these signals without automatically assuming they're dangerous. Instead of reacting with panic or shutting down, you'll learn to observe with curiosity and respond with intention.

This process isn't based on guesswork—it's grounded in neuroscience. Our brains are designed to track both internal and external cues. When we engage with these cues mindfully and consistently, we begin to reshape the brain's response to stress, creating new pathways for regulation, resilience, and calm. Attunement in therapy creates the foundation for emotional safety. When you feel understood and accepted by your therapist, it becomes easier to develop that same understanding toward yourself. Learning attunement is a relational and internal process—both matter.

This work takes time. Attunement is not something you "master" in a day—it's something we build together through repetition, trust, and awareness. Over time, you will come to recognize your patterns, feel more grounded in your experiences, and understand what healthy self-connection feels like. And that, in itself, is a powerful turning point in anxiety recovery.

Foundational Needs: The Role of Physical Health in Anxiety Recovery

Psychologist Abraham Maslow's research on human needs emphasizes that basic survival factors must be addressed before higher-level emotional and psychological healing can take place. If fundamental needs—such as nutrition, hydration, sleep, and overall physical well-being—are neglected, anxiety work becomes significantly more difficult.

The mind and body are deeply connected. Research has shown that nutritional deficiencies, chronic stress, poor sleep, and hormonal imbalances can all contribute to increased anxiety, depression, and cognitive challenges. For instance, low levels of vitamin B have been linked to heightened anxiety, while dehydration can worsen fatigue and brain fog, making it harder to manage stress.

Because of this, we take a comprehensive look at foundational health factors early in therapy. A health screening tool is used to assess whether physical imbalances may be contributing to emotional distress. Addressing these underlying physical factors doesn't replace anxiety work, but it makes it far more effective. Simple adjustments—such as improving nutrition, establishing healthier sleep patterns, or managing chronic pain—can provide the stability needed to fully engage in the deeper psychological work ahead.

Why This Step Matters

Many individuals struggling with anxiety want to jump straight into addressing anxious thoughts and emotions without first ensuring they have the stability to do so. However, without a sense of safety and attention to basic physiological needs, deeper anxiety work can quickly become overwhelming, frustrating, or even ineffective.

Establishing trusting connections and addressing physical well-being creates the necessary conditions for progress. This is why Level One focuses on building safe connections and stabilizing foundational needs—ensuring that when we move into more advanced anxiety work, we have the security and resilience to engage with it effectively and sustainably

Discomfort Does Not Always Mean Something Is Wrong

One of the most important lessons in anxiety recovery is learning that discomfort does not automatically signal that something is wrong. Your nervous system may interpret new, uncertain, or emotionally vulnerable situations as threatening—not because they are harmful, but because they are unfamiliar or difficult to control.

This is a natural response, especially if past experiences have reinforced the idea that being uncomfortable means you're failing, at risk of judgment, or out of control.

Part of our work together is helping you differentiate between actual misalignment and the temporary discomfort that comes from doing something new or challenging—experiences that often support growth, not hinder it.

I encourage you to speak up when you feel uncomfortable. That discomfort is not a problem to avoid—it's information. It helps us understand where you are and what support you need. Therapy is not about rushing or forcing change; it's about building trust at a sustainable pace.

How Anxiety Leads to Avoidance

When discomfort arises, it's natural to want to pull away or disengage from therapy. These avoidance responses are often automatic self-protection mechanisms that have developed over time. However, avoiding discomfort can reinforce anxiety, keeping you stuck in old patterns rather than helping you move forward.

Here are some common ways anxiety-driven discomfort can lead to withdrawal from therapy:

- **Fleeing:** Feeling the urge to leave a session, cancel future appointments, or avoid therapy altogether to escape uncomfortable emotions or topics.
- **Convincing yourself you don't need therapy:** Telling yourself, *"I'm fine"* or *"I don't need help"* to avoid the vulnerability of deeper self-exploration.
- **Minimizing or distorting the truth:** Downplaying your struggles or not fully opening up about what's going on to avoid feeling exposed.
- **Avoiding difficult topics:** Skipping over key issues, changing the subject, or becoming defensive when certain subjects arise.
- **Shutting down:** Becoming emotionally numb, disengaged, or disconnected rather than processing the emotions that surface.
- **Self-sabotaging:** Finding excuses not to follow through with assignments, exercises, or therapy goals as a way to avoid deeper discomfort.

Facing Discomfort as a Path to Growth

Recognizing these patterns is an important part of healing. Together, we will work to understand what triggers these responses and develop strategies to move through them rather than avoid them.

Your discomfort is not a sign of failure—it's often an indicator that change is happening. When approached with curiosity and patience, discomfort becomes a signal for growth rather than a reason to withdraw.

Assignment 1: Letter to Your Therapist
What You Should Know

This exercise gives you a chance to reflect on how you experience connection, communication, and trust, especially in a therapeutic setting. Many individuals living with anxiety develop subtle, often unseen ways of managing discomfort in relationships. These adaptations can impact how you show up in sessions—whether through overexplaining, hesitating to share, or scanning for approval.

This letter is your opportunity to help me understand what feels supportive to you and what may create tension or anxiety in our work together. Consider the following prompts as you write:

- How do you typically respond in new or unfamiliar relationships?
- Are there certain behaviors you use to manage anxiety in conversations or social settings? (e.g., over-apologizing, mentally rehearsing what to say, withdrawing when overwhelmed)
- What kinds of therapist responses or environments help you feel more at ease?
- Are there things that make it harder for you to speak freely or be honest in a session?
- What do you hope I will understand about how anxiety affects the way you relate to others—and to yourself?

This letter isn't about justifying your behavior or getting it "right." It's about making therapy a place where you can feel safe enough to be real. The more we understand your internal experience, the better we can support your process.

DEAR THERAPIST,
WHAT YOU SHOULD KNOW-

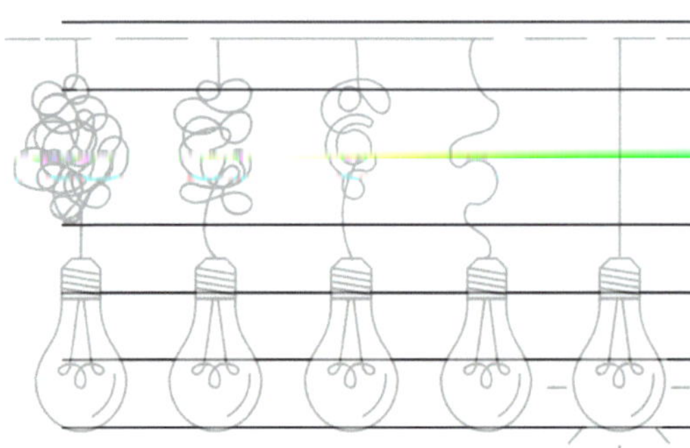

Assignment 2: Attunement in Practice- Mirroring

Once foundational trust is in place, we'll begin exploring attunement in real time. One way we do this is through a process called mirroring—a natural, often unconscious part of human connection where we begin to reflect each other's posture, tone, or gestures. In therapy, this can be used intentionally to help you become more aware of your own internal cues and how connection with others affects your sense of safety and regulation.

Mirroring Hand Movement Exercise

1. Sit across from me in session (or try this with a trusted person).
2. I will move my hand slowly in different directions, keeping my movements smooth and natural.
3. You will follow along, mirroring the movement exactly.
4. After a few minutes, we will switch roles.
5. Afterward, we will reflect on how this experience felt.

This exercise engages mirror neurons, which help our brain recognize connection, trust, and co-regulation. While it may feel unnatural at first, these small, safe interactions help build relational confidence and emotional awareness over time.

Additional Attunement Practice: Sensory Awareness Check-In

Because anxiety tends to heighten awareness of physical sensations, this check-in is designed to help you observe your body's responses without judgment. Rather than interpreting every sensation as a warning sign, this is an opportunity to build familiarity with your internal cues in a calm and grounded way.

- Take a breath and bring gentle attention to your body.
- What do you notice—tightness, stillness, fidgeting, holding your breath?
- Are certain parts of your body more activated than others?
- As I speak or guide an exercise, do you feel more at ease or more tense?
- Are there moments where you feel neutral, safe, or unexpectedly calm?
- Quietly name what you're experiencing—no need to explain, just acknowledge it

Note:
You might feel a little uncomfortable with this at first—and that's completely normal. You may find yourself thinking, *"Is this really therapy?"* or *"Why does this feel awkward?"* The truth is, this type of real-time interaction is both intentional and supported by neuroscience. It's designed to help strengthen your awareness, connection, and regulation.

Assignment 3:
Foundational Needs- Whole Health Screening

As part of our work together, you will complete a Health Screening Tool to help identify whether any physical factors may be contributing to your anxiety. This screening is not diagnostic, but it can bring attention to areas that may need further exploration—such as nutritional deficiencies, sleep issues, chronic pain, or hormonal imbalances. If concerns emerge, we may discuss the benefit of consulting with a medical provider, such as a primary care physician, endocrinologist, or nutritionist. While referrals will be offered thoughtfully, outcomes with external providers are beyond our scope of control.

Note:
The health screening will be completed during a session if you are working with a therapist at Untangled Mind. If you are using this workbook independently, the screening tool can still serve as a valuable resource. Consider bringing it to your primary care provider or another healthcare professional to support a more informed discussion about your overall well-being.

Whether in therapy or on your own, self-advocacy is a vital part of your healing journey. Understanding and communicating your physical and emotional needs helps ensure that you receive the support you deserve. This screening is one step toward viewing anxiety recovery through a whole-person lens—recognizing that your mind and body are deeply connected.

Health Screening Checklist

I. General Health Status

☐ Do you currently have a primary care physician?
☐ When was your last physical exam?
Date:
☐ Have you had a full blood panel done in the past year?
☐ Are you currently taking any prescribed or over-the-counter medications?
List:
☐ Any recent hospitalizations, surgeries, or significant health events?
Explain:
☐ Do you have any known medical conditions?
List:
☐ Have you had any unexplained weight loss or gain in the past year?

II. Blood Panel & Metabolic Health

☐ Have you had your hormone levels checked in the past year? (e.g., thyroid, testosterone, estrogen, cortisol)
☐ Have you had your thyroid function checked? (TSH, Free T3, Free T4, Thyroid Antibodies)
☐ Have you had your vitamin and mineral levels checked? (Vitamin D, B12, Iron, Magnesium, Folate)
☐ Have you had a cholesterol panel in the past year? (HDL, LDL, Triglycerides)
☐ Have you had your blood sugar levels checked? (Fasting glucose, A1C)
☐ Have you had kidney and liver function tests?
☐ Have you been checked for autoimmune conditions (e.g., lupus, rheumatoid arthritis, Hashimoto's, celiac disease)?

III. Sleep & Rest

☐ Do you sleep at least 7-9 hours per night?
☐ Do you have difficulty falling asleep or staying asleep?
☐ Do you feel well-rested upon waking?
☐ Do you experience excessive fatigue during the day?
☐ Have you been assessed for sleep disorders (e.g., sleep apnea, restless leg syndrome)?

IV. Nutrition & Hydration

☐ Do you eat at least three balanced meals per day?
☐ Do you consume enough protein, healthy fats, and fiber?

☐ Do you experience frequent digestive issues (bloating, reflux, constipation, diarrhea)?
☐ Have you been diagnosed with IBS, Crohn's, or other GI conditions?
☐ Do you experience frequent heartburn or acid reflux?
☐ Do you drink at least 64 oz of water daily?
☐ Do you consume excessive caffeine, sugar, or processed foods?

V. Physical Activity & Musculoskeletal Health

☐ Do you engage in at least 30 minutes of physical activity most days of the week?
☐ Do you feel physically strong and capable of performing daily tasks?
☐ Do you experience chronic pain, stiffness, or joint discomfort?
☐ Have you had any recent injuries, fractures, or surgeries?
☐ Do you have any known spinal, joint, or muscular issues? (e.g., herniated disc, arthritis, fibromyalgia)
☐ Do you experience frequent headaches or migraines?

VI. Stress, Cognition & Nervous System Health

☐ Do you experience frequent headaches, muscle tension, or body aches?
☐ Have you noticed changes in memory, focus, or mental clarity?
☐ Do you frequently feel brain fog or trouble concentrating?
☐ Have you experienced dizziness, vertigo, or balance issues?
☐ Have you had a concussion or head injury in the past?
☐ Have you been diagnosed with neurological conditions (e.g., epilepsy, MS, Parkinson's)?

VII. Substance Use & Lifestyle Factors

☐ Do you currently or have you ever used tobacco/nicotine products?
If yes, how often?
☐ Do you consume alcohol?
If yes, how often?
☐ Do you use recreational drugs or substances?
If yes, which and how often?
☐ Have you been diagnosed with or suspected of having a substance use disorder?
☐ Have you ever been prescribed medications for anxiety, depression, or ADHD?
List:

VIII. Shelter, Safety & Environmental Health

☐ Do you have stable and safe housing?
☐ Do you feel secure in your home environment?
☐ Do you have access to heating/cooling, clean water, and electricity?
☐ Do you have regular access to nutritious food?
☐ Have you experienced domestic violence, abuse, or unsafe living conditions?

IX. Additional Health Concerns

☐ Do you experience frequent infections or immune system issues?
☐ Have you had unusual skin changes, rashes, or hair loss?
☐ Do you experience chronic nausea, dizziness, or unexplained pain?
☐ Do you have hearing or vision concerns?
☐ Have you had any recent unexplained medical symptoms.

X. Next Steps & Referrals

☐ Referral to Primary Care Physician
☐ Referral to Endocrinologist for Hormone/Thyroid Check
☐ Referral to Gastroenterologist for Digestive Concerns
☐ Referral to Sleep Specialist
☐ Referral to Neurologist for Cognitive Concerns
☐ Referral for Blood Work & Metabolic Panel
☐ Referral to Nutritionist/Dietitian
☐ Referral for Substance Use Evaluation
☐ Other:

Therapist Check In

Activity	Date Completed	Client Initials	Therapist Initials
A1: Letter: What You Should Know			
A2: Attunement			
A3: Whole Health Screening			

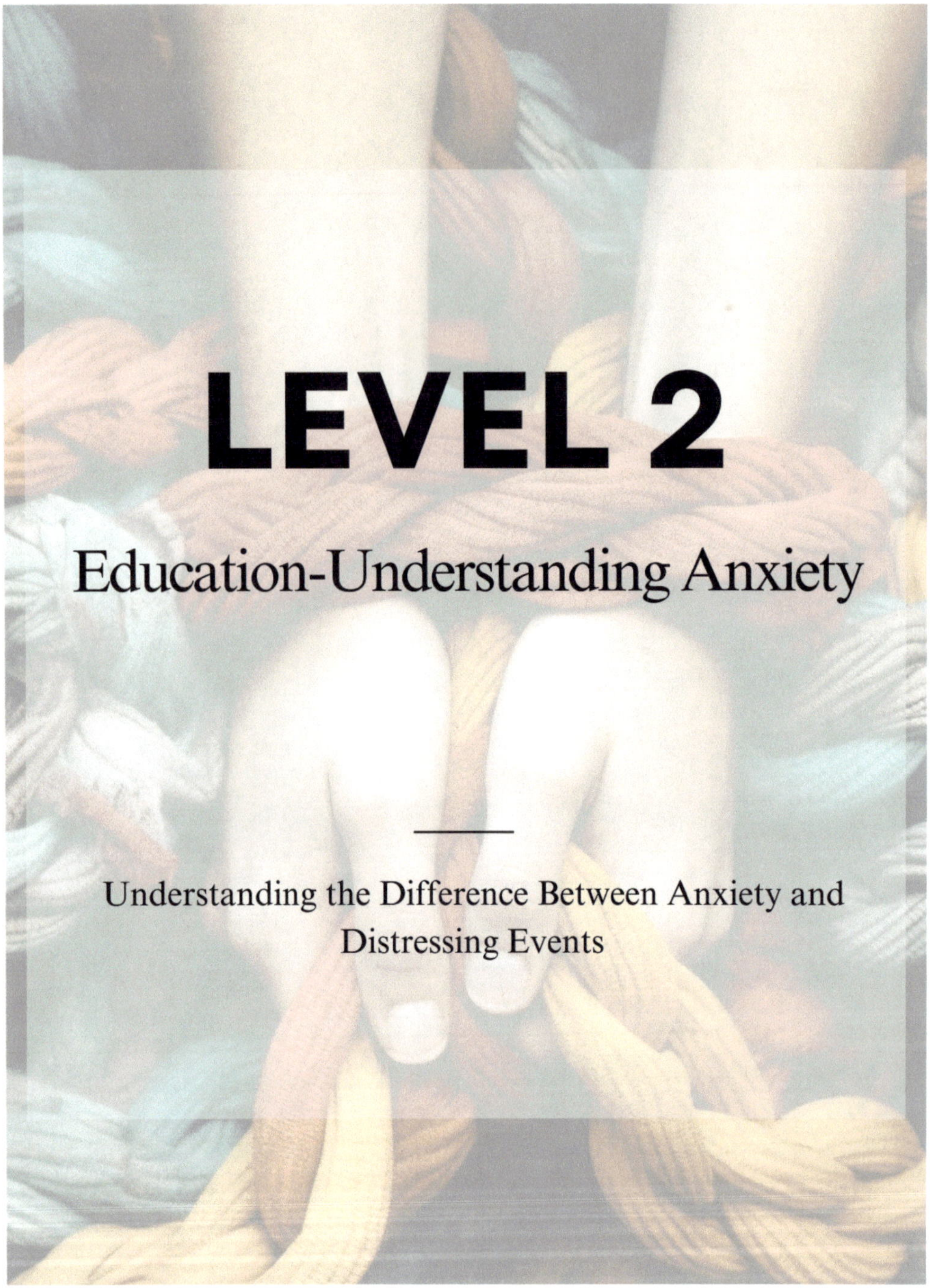

LEVEL 2

Education-Understanding Anxiety

Understanding the Difference Between Anxiety and Distressing Events

The Essential Role of Education in Anxiety Recovery

Education is a critical component of anxiety recovery. Without a clear understanding of what anxiety is and how it affects the brain, body, and memory, individuals often feel lost, ashamed, or frustrated by their own experiences. Many people struggling with anxiety blame themselves for their symptoms, believing something is fundamentally "wrong" with them—but knowledge changes that.

When you learn how your nervous system responds to anxiety, why triggers feel overwhelming, and how your brain processes and recalls anxious experiences differently, you begin to see your struggles in a new light. Education provides language for what often feels chaotic and uncontrollable, replacing self-judgment with understanding. Instead of defaulting to labels like *"I'm broken"* or *"I'm just overreacting,"* you'll gain clarity on why your body and mind react the way they do—and how to work with those responses rather than against them.

Including anxiety education as part of Foundational Needs ensures that recovery is not just about coping with symptoms but about understanding what's happening beneath them. Anxiety-informed education reduces fear, normalizes experiences, and provides a roadmap for healing. When you can name what's happening, you can take active steps to change it. Understanding anxiety isn't just about acquiring facts—it's about reclaiming power, shifting perspectives, and building confidence to move forward in healing.

Note: Why Education is Central to Untangled Mind's Approach

At Untangled Mind, our philosophy is centered on equipping you with every possible tool to support your healing journey. Education is one of the most powerful tools available, yet many therapy approaches overlook or undervalue its role.

Our goal is not just to provide you with knowledge but to ensure that you fully understand the key principles of anxiety recovery and gain practical tools that allow you to build autonomy in your life. Therapy should empower you, not create dependence. We want you to walk away from this process with more than just insight—we want you to have the confidence and ability to apply what you've learned, making lasting changes and taking ownership of your healing journey.

What Is Anxiety?

Anxiety is a natural and necessary response to stress, but when it becomes persistent, excessive, or difficult to control, it can interfere with daily life. Unlike temporary worry or nervousness, clinical anxiety involves emotional, physical, and cognitive responses that are heightened and often disproportionate to the actual situation.

This workbook is designed for individuals who experience ongoing anxiety that causes significant distress and interferes with daily life. While anxiety can look different from person to person, the tools offered here are meant to support those who struggle with persistent worry, internal tension, and patterns of avoidance or over-control that feel difficult to manage.

You may find yourself:

- Constantly anticipating worst-case scenarios
- Overthinking decisions or replaying conversations
- Feeling physically tense, restless, or keyed up
- Avoiding certain situations to prevent anxious discomfort
- Struggling to relax, even when circumstances seem calm

Although there are different types of anxiety with specific clinical names, this workbook does not focus on diagnosis or labels. Instead, it provides evidence-based tools and structured guidance to help you understand your anxiety patterns, build emotional regulation, and create meaningful, sustainable change. Whether your anxiety has been a long-standing pattern or a more recent experience, the goal of this workbook is to help you regain clarity, confidence, and a sense of control.

Why Understanding Anxiety Matters

When you live with anxiety, it can be easy to believe that your reactions are irrational, excessive, or somehow your fault. Many individuals internalize their symptoms as flaws in character or strength. But anxiety isn't a personal failure—it's a learned and reinforced pattern of mental, emotional, and physical responses that can be understood and reshaped.

By gaining insight into:

- How anxiety impacts the brain and nervous system
- Why anxious thoughts feel urgent and difficult to ignore
- How habits like overthinking, avoidance, or control reinforce anxiety

...you begin to build a new relationship with anxiety—one based on awareness and choice, rather than fear or confusion. Education is a foundational step in recovery, and this workbook will guide you through practical, evidence-informed strategies to interrupt anxiety patterns and foster lasting resilience.

Why It's Important to Understand the Difference

In today's culture, it's common to hear people casually use psychological terms—"I'm so OCD," "I have trauma," or "I'm just an anxious person." While these phrases may reflect moments of stress or overwhelm, they can blur the line between temporary emotional states and clinically significant patterns. The risk in using diagnostic language loosely is that we may start to internalize labels that don't truly reflect what we're experiencing—and in doing so, limit our growth.

It's important to understand the difference between feeling upset, which is a normal and healthy emotional response to life's challenges, and anxiety, which involves a persistent, patterned response that often feels hard to turn off. Recognizing this difference allows you to respond more effectively to what you're feeling—without over-pathologizing yourself or ignoring signs that more support may be needed.

The following table outlines key differences between upset and anxiety, offering language to help you better interpret your experience without getting stuck in unhelpful labels.

Understanding the Difference

Upset	Anxiety
Triggered by a specific situation	May not have an obvious trigger or worry shifts between topics
Emotional intensity decreases over time	Worry and discomfort persist, often escalating
Feelings align with the actual situation	Worry is often disproportionate or hypothetical
Can be resolved through problem-solving	Often involves rumination and "what-if" thinking
Does not significantly disrupt daily life	Can interfere with work, relationships, and overall well-being

Recognizing the difference between anxiety and general upset is essential for navigating your emotions effectively. By understanding when worry becomes excessive or disproportionate, you can begin to apply targeted strategies to regain a sense of control.

How Anxiety Develops Over Time

Anxiety can emerge in different ways depending on life experiences, stress levels, and personal coping mechanisms. For some, anxiety may arise suddenly due to a major life event, while for others, it may develop gradually over time due to ongoing stress or uncertainty. Understanding how your anxiety has taken shape can help guide the most effective strategies for managing it.

Patterns of Anxiety Development

1. **Situational Anxiety (Short-Term Anxiety Response)**
    - Triggered by a specific stressor, such as a major life change, job loss, or health scare.
    - Symptoms spike in intensity but may lessen as the situation stabilizes.

2. **Persistent Anxiety (Long-Term Generalized Anxiety)**
    - Worry and stress are ongoing, not tied to one specific event, and often shift between different concerns (work, relationships, health, etc.).
    - Commonly associated with Generalized Anxiety Disorder (GAD) and may include chronic muscle tension, restlessness, sleep disturbances, and difficulty concentrating.
    - Anxiety remains even when external circumstances improve, indicating that the worry is not solely situational but part of a broader pattern.

3. **Cumulative Anxiety (Lifelong Sensitivity to Stress)**
    - Anxiety builds over time due to repeated exposure to stress, high expectations, or unstable environments.
    - Often involves early learned patterns of excessive worry, hyper-responsibility, or difficulty managing uncertainty.
    - May include a combination of situational and persistent anxiety, making it harder to pinpoint a single root cause.

Why Identifying Your Anxiety Pattern Matters

Anxiety is not a one-size-fits-all experience. For some, it's tied to a specific event. For others, it becomes a long-standing presence that weaves into daily life. In many cases, anxiety builds slowly over time—layered by repeated stress, self-doubt, or constant overthinking. Understanding how your anxiety shows up can help you choose the most effective strategies for managing it.

- Situational Anxiety – Triggered by a specific event or temporary stressor, and usually fades when the situation resolves. It often responds well to short-term coping tools like grounding, reframing, and structured problem-solving.
- Persistent Anxiety – A steady presence over time, often unrelated to external events. This pattern benefits from consistent tools such as thought restructuring, habit interruption, and behavioral change.
- Chronic or Cumulative Anxiety – Built up over years through repeated stress, uncertainty, or deeply ingrained thinking patterns. Recovery here involves unlearning automatic responses, strengthening emotional regulation, and shifting long-held beliefs that reinforce the anxious cycle.

You don't need a diagnosis to benefit from understanding your pattern. Naming what you're experiencing gives you clarity—and clarity gives you choices.

Why the Word "Anxiety" Might Not Resonate

For many people, especially those in high-performing, caregiving, or leadership roles, what we call "anxiety" often feels like just life. Feeling the pressure to meet deadlines, take care of others, anticipate problems, or avoid mistakes becomes part of how we function. Over time, this constant vigilance and forward-focus can become so normal that we don't even question it—we just keep pushing.

In fact, parts of anxiety may even serve us well. It can drive preparation, motivate performance, or help us avoid failure. If you've told yourself, *"I work better under pressure"* or *"Worrying is how I stay in control,"* you're not alone. For many, anxiety is not an unfamiliar foe—it's a well-worn strategy for navigating a demanding world.

But here's the key: naming anxiety doesn't mean you're weak—it means you're ready to challenge it. By identifying what anxiety is doing—both the helpful and harmful—you begin to take control, rather than letting it quietly control you. This workbook is not about labeling you. It's about helping you look at the patterns you've developed, understand why they exist, and decide which ones you want to keep—and which ones you're ready to outgrow.

Assignment 1: Defining Your Experience

1. **Describe an event or experience that you initially believed was caused by anxiety.** Think about a moment where you felt unsettled, overwhelmed, or emotionally activated. What happened? What thoughts or physical sensations did you notice?

2. **Reflect on that experience using what you've learned about anxiety so far.** Based on the definitions and distinctions we've explored, do you believe your response was rooted in a persistent anxiety pattern, or was it more of a situational emotional reaction? Explain your reasoning.

3. **How does seeing this experience through a more informed lens affect your emotional response or self-perception?**
   Has your understanding of the experience shifted? Do you feel more empowered, more compassionate toward yourself, or more aware of how you tend to react?

The Impact of Anxiety

Anxiety affects us on multiple levels, influencing how we think, feel, and respond to daily life. Recognizing these effects can help you understand your experience and begin to take steps toward managing your anxiety more effectively.

- **Cognitively:** Anxiety can distort thought patterns, leading to excessive worry, difficulty concentrating, or an ongoing sense of dread. It may cause overthinking, rumination, or a heightened focus on potential problems.
- **Emotionally:** Feelings of nervousness, unease, irritability, or restlessness may become persistent. Anxiety can also create a sense of emotional exhaustion, making it harder to regulate mood or feel at ease.
- **Physically:** Anxiety triggers the body's stress response, often leading to muscle tension, fatigue, headaches, sleep disturbances, digestive issues, or rapid heartbeat. Chronic anxiety can make it difficult to relax, even in low-stress situations.

The Anxiety Cycle

Anxiety often follows a predictable cycle, reinforcing itself over time. Recognizing this cycle can help you identify where to intervene and make meaningful changes.

- **Triggers:** Events, thoughts, sensations, or situations that provoke anxious responses. These may be external (e.g., an upcoming deadline or social interaction) or internal (e.g., self-doubt or bodily sensations like a racing heart).
- **Thoughts:** Anxiety is often accompanied by excessive worry, intrusive thoughts, or cognitive distortions such as catastrophizing (*"What if something terrible happens?"*) or all-or-nothing thinking (*"If I can't do it perfectly, I shouldn't do it at all."*).
- **Feelings:** Anxiety creates intense emotional responses, including nervousness, irritability, dread, or fear. These emotions fuel the anxious cycle and can feel difficult to control.
- **Behaviors:** In response to anxiety, individuals may engage in avoidance (steering clear of feared situations), reassurance-seeking (relying on others to confirm everything is okay), procrastination (delaying tasks due to fear of failure), or excessive control-seeking (trying to eliminate uncertainty). These behaviors temporarily relieve anxiety but reinforce the cycle in the long run.

Understanding this cycle is the first step toward breaking free from unhelpful patterns. By recognizing how anxiety progresses, you can learn to challenge anxious thoughts, develop healthier responses, and gradually reduce its impact on your daily life.

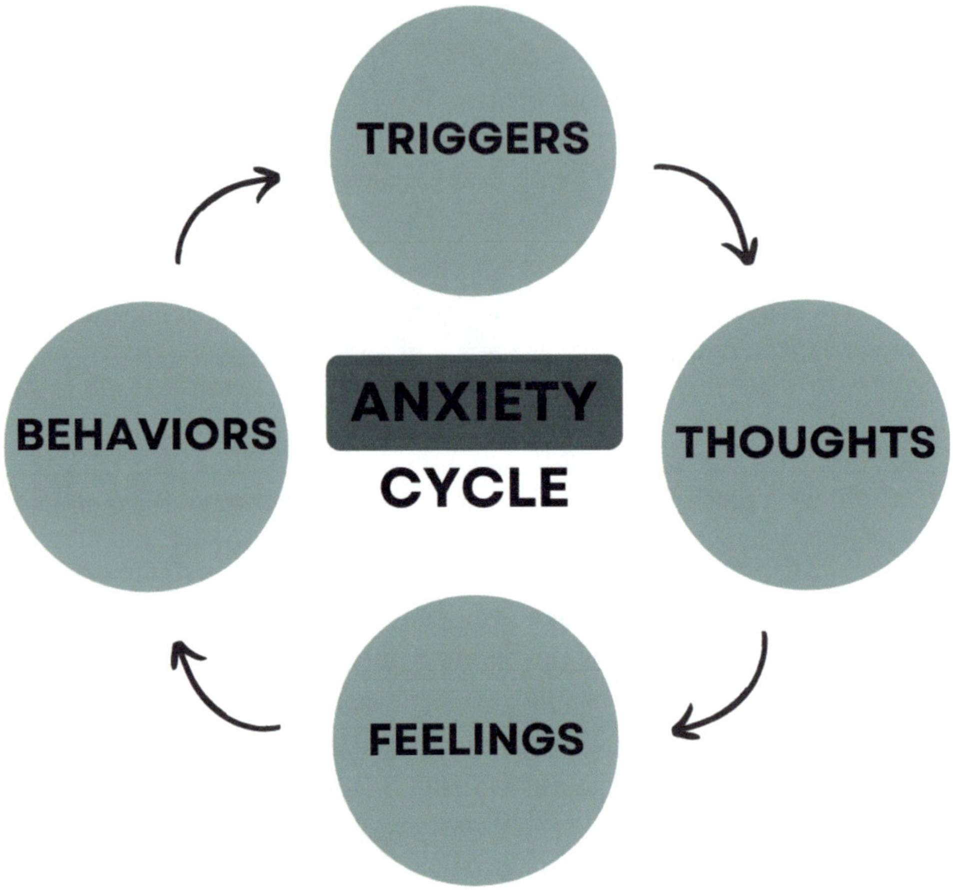
TRIGGERS
THOUGHTS
FEELINGS
BEHAVIORS
ANXIETY
CYCLE

Assignment 2: Mapping Your Anxiety Cycle

Take a moment to reflect on a recent experience where you felt a strong reaction related to anxiety. Map the following:

- **Trigger**: What prompted your response?

- **Thoughts**: What went through your mind?

- **Feelings**: How did you feel emotionally?

- **Behaviors**: What actions or reactions followed?

Assignment 3: Understanding Your Anxiety Pattern

Anxiety is not one-size-fits-all—it can develop in different ways depending on life experiences, stressors, and individual coping mechanisms. In this assignment, you will identify three life events and categorize them into one of the following three areas:

1. **Situational Anxiety** – Anxiety triggered by a specific event or temporary stressor.
2. **Persistent Anxiety** – Anxiety that remains consistent over time, regardless of immediate circumstances.
3. **Cumulative Anxiety** – Anxiety that develops gradually due to long-term stressors or repeated patterns of worry.

Understanding how your anxiety presents can help you recognize which areas need attention and what strategies may be most effective for you.

1. Situational Anxiety

Situational anxiety occurs in response to a specific stressor and typically subsides once the situation is resolved. This type of anxiety may feel overwhelming in the moment but does not necessarily persist long-term.

Examples: Preparing for an important presentation, going through a breakup, awaiting medical test results, adjusting to a major life change.

How it affects you: You may experience short-term physical symptoms (such as tension, nausea, or restlessness) and cognitive symptoms (such as racing thoughts or difficulty focusing). Once the situation improves, symptoms tend to lessen or disappear.

2. Persistent Anxiety

Persistent anxiety is ongoing and not tied to a single event. It often involves excessive worry across multiple areas of life, making it difficult to pinpoint a specific trigger.

Examples: Constant worry about finances, health, relationships, or work, even when things are going well. Feeling on edge most of the time without an identifiable cause.

How it affects you: Symptoms may include chronic muscle tension, irritability, sleep disturbances, and difficulty controlling worry, even when there's no immediate threat or stressor.

3. Cumulative Anxiety

Cumulative anxiety develops gradually across the lifespan due to repeated exposure to chronic stress, emotionally demanding environments, or ongoing uncertainty. Rather than being tied to one event or season of life, it is shaped by a consistent pattern of pressure, vigilance, or unmet emotional needs that condition the nervous system to stay in a heightened state of alert.

Examples: Growing up in a high-pressure or emotionally unpredictable household, managing long-term caregiving responsibilities, navigating chronic work stress, or facing ongoing instability in relationships or finances.

How it affects you: Symptoms may include heightened sensitivity to stress, difficulty relaxing even in safe or calm environments, a tendency to over-prepare or overthink, and a constant underlying sense that something could go wrong. This form of anxiety often feels deeply embedded and automatic, as if it's simply "how you are."

Assignment Instructions

1. **Identify three life events or patterns** that have contributed to your anxiety.
2. **Categorize** each one as Situational Anxiety, Persistent Anxiety, or Cumulative Anxiety, using the descriptions above.
3. **Reflect on how these patterns affect you:**
   - Do you notice a theme in how your anxiety develops?
   - Have some of these experiences reinforced or worsened your anxiety over time?
   - Are there certain strategies that help with situational anxiety but don't work for persistent or cumulative anxiety?

The Venn Diagram: Identifying Overlap

As you fill in your Venn diagram, consider how these categories may overlap:

- Where Situational Anxiety and Persistent Anxiety overlap: A stressful event may initially trigger situational anxiety, but if worry continues long after the event, it may develop into persistent anxiety.
- Where Persistent Anxiety and Cumulative Anxiety overlap: Long-term, repeated exposure to stress may reinforce persistent worry, making anxiety feel like a default state rather than a temporary reaction.
- The Middle Overlap (All Three Categories): Some experiences may feel situational at first, turn into persistent worry, and eventually contribute to a cumulative anxiety pattern over time.

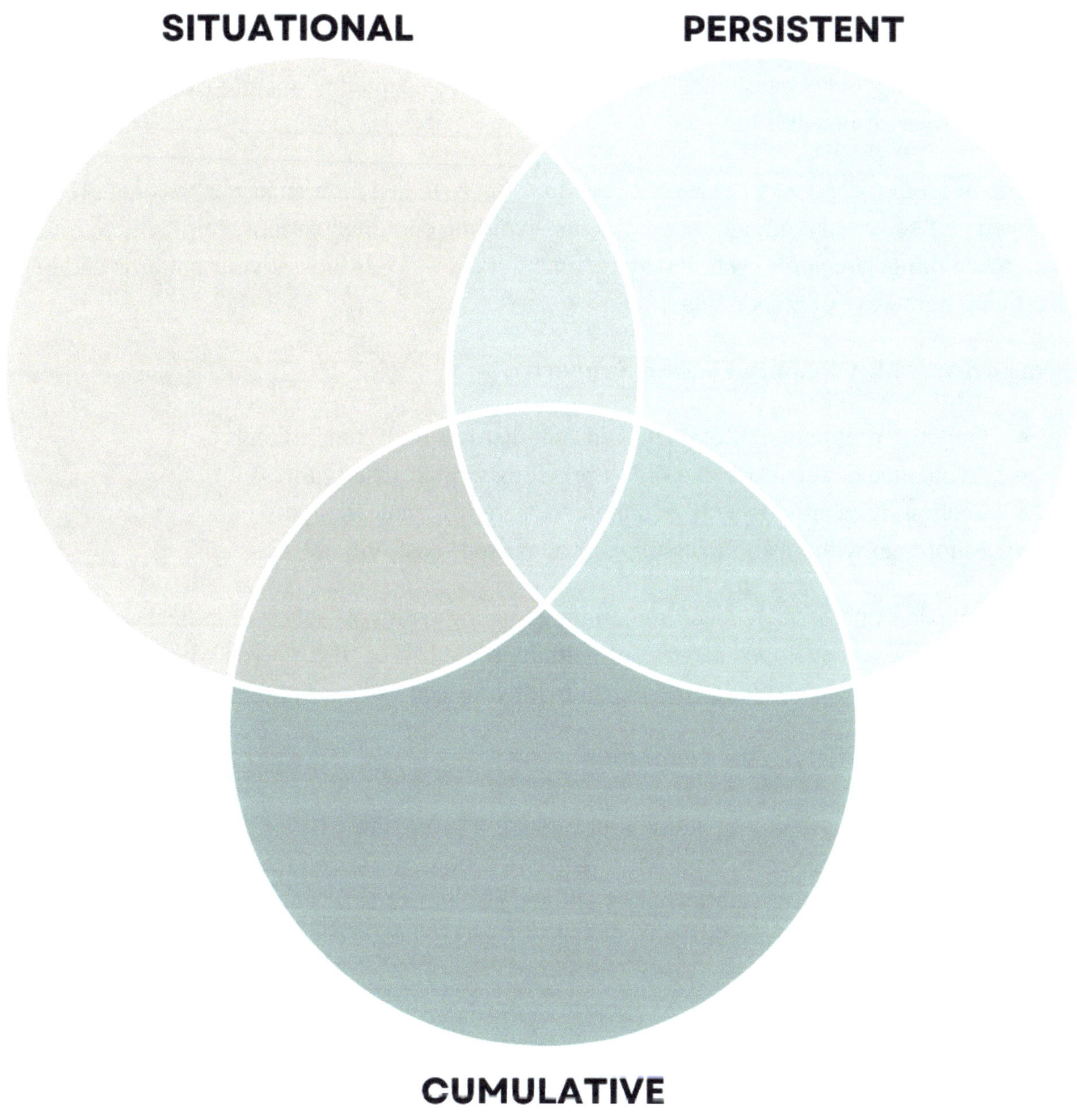
SITUATIONAL
PERSISTENT
CUMULATIVE

Moving Beyond the Anxiety Cycle

Anxiety is a natural response to stress and uncertainty, but when it becomes ongoing and unmanageable, it can begin to interfere with your daily life, relationships, and sense of well-being. Many people remain stuck in an anxiety cycle for years—not because they're doing something wrong, but because their brain and body have adapted to operate from a place of fear, control, or over-responsibility.

It's important to recognize when anxiety becomes more than a momentary experience. If you find yourself constantly anticipating problems, avoiding certain situations, or unable to relax even when things are going well, it may be time to take a closer look at your patterns and begin practicing new ways of responding.

Signs Anxiety May Require Focused Support

- Ongoing rumination or overanalysis that disrupts daily functioning
- Avoidance of situations that didn't previously cause discomfort
- Feeling frequently on edge or unable to "turn off" your thoughts
- Emotional withdrawal, irritability, or increased sensitivity to stress

These signs don't necessarily mean something is wrong with you—they're indications that your nervous system has developed patterns of reacting to perceived threat, even when no real danger is present. The goal isn't to judge these patterns, but to understand and retrain them.

Understanding Anxiety as an Adaptation

Anxiety isn't weakness—it's a pattern your mind and body learned over time. While those patterns may have once served a purpose, they can become rigid and reactive, keeping you stuck. Healing doesn't mean eliminating anxiety altogether—it means learning how to respond to it with clarity, intention, and confidence.

Assignment 4: Identifying Anxiety Narratives

Why This Assignment Matters:

The way we think about anxiety—where it comes from, what it means, and how we're supposed to deal with it—is often shaped long before we experience it directly. Family messages, cultural values, professional norms, and media portrayals all influence how we understand anxiety and respond to it. These messages create powerful narratives that, over time, can either support or hinder our ability to manage anxiety effectively.

For example, if you grew up in an environment where emotional expression was seen as weakness, you may feel shame or frustration when anxiety shows up. If you've absorbed the belief that anxiety only counts when it's linked to extreme or life-threatening events, you might minimize your own distress and avoid seeking help. Even workplace or community cultures that normalize chronic stress can lead you to ignore signs that something needs attention.

When left unexamined, these narratives can reinforce distorted thinking—fueling avoidance, self-blame, perfectionism, or emotional suppression. But once you identify and question them, you begin to regain authorship over your story. This assignment is not about blaming your past. It's about becoming aware of the beliefs you've carried and deciding which ones you want to continue—and which you're ready to let go.

Journal:
Explore a cultural or personal narrative about anxiety that has influenced your beliefs.
How do societal messages about anxiety impact *your* healing process?

Journal: Anxiety Narratives

Choose a **personal, cultural, or family belief** about anxiety that has shaped how you view yourself or your struggles.

1. What was the message?

2. How did it influence your understanding of anxiety?

3. Does it help or hinder your recovery today?

4. What belief would you like to hold instead?

Growth Beyond Anxiety: Resilience, Grit, and Psychological Strength

Living with anxiety—especially when it is chronic or cumulative—can feel exhausting. It affects how you think, relate, and respond to the world. But what's often overlooked is this: working through anxiety can also strengthen you. While anxiety is not something we seek out or celebrate, facing it intentionally can lead to meaningful psychological growth.

Unlike short-term coping, this growth is not just about surviving anxious moments. It's about building grit (the perseverance to keep going despite emotional discomfort), cultivating resilience (the ability to recover and adapt), and deepening self-awareness that leads to lasting change.

This isn't a toxic positivity message—healing from anxiety is not about "just being stronger." It's about doing the difficult work of noticing your patterns, challenging your thinking, staying engaged with your values, and showing up for your life with intention. This type of growth often comes in subtle ways and over time. But the outcome? A more grounded, confident version of yourself who knows how to face discomfort without losing clarity or purpose.

Key Areas Where Growth Can Occur

New Perspectives and Mental Flexibility:
Living with anxiety often pushes people to become deeply reflective. Many individuals begin to shift their focus from avoiding discomfort to navigating it with purpose. Priorities change. What once felt urgent may no longer carry the same weight, and values like rest, connection, or meaning begin to take precedence.

Increased Resilience and Inner Strength:
As you learn to face and regulate your anxiety, you may discover a capacity for strength you didn't know existed. Over time, anxiety becomes less of a threat and more of a signal—something to work with rather than run from. This shift builds confidence, self-trust, and emotional endurance.

Purpose Through Challenge:
When you do the work of understanding your anxiety, new meaning often emerges. You might find purpose in helping others, setting boundaries that honor your mental health, or pursuing goals once held back by fear. Grit research shows that sustained effort through difficulty builds both competence and a sense of fulfillment.

Stronger Relationships and Empathy:
The path through anxiety often deepens emotional insight. Many people become more attuned to their needs and more empathetic toward others. As shame and avoidance decrease, vulnerability and honesty grow—allowing for more connected and supportive relationships.

Reclaiming Identity and Agency:
Anxiety can distort how you see yourself—limiting your sense of what's possible. Growth involves recognizing that you are not your symptoms. Through skill-building, emotional regulation, and reframing, you begin to reclaim your role as the decision-maker in your life. This process restores agency and helps you move forward with confidence, even when anxiety shows up.

Moving Beyond Coping

Coping helps us get through the moment. But growth changes how we show up for life. This workbook is not just about reducing symptoms—it's about equipping you to shift your mindset, reclaim your choices, and build a life that isn't dictated by fear.

Growth through anxiety doesn't happen all at once. It happens in quiet moments—when you challenge a thought instead of spiraling, when you take a risk that used to terrify you, when you sit with discomfort and choose not to run from it. These are the moments that lead to transformation.

Assignment 5: Timeline of Resilience

1. **Identify several moments in your life where you faced a meaningful challenge—emotionally, mentally, or circumstantially.**
   These don't need to be dramatic or traumatic events. They can include times of sustained stress, transition, uncertainty, or inner struggle. List the approximate dates and a brief description of each experience.

2. **Reflect on how you moved through those moments.**
   What helped you cope at the time? What did you learn about yourself? Consider any skills, mindsets, or values that began to form or strengthen as a result. Write about how those experiences shaped your resilience or sense of identity.

3. **Now, connect your past to your present.**
   In what ways can the strengths you've developed help you face your anxiety today? How might remembering your capacity for growth reframe how you approach your current challenges?

Therapist Check In

Activity	Date Completed	Client Initials	Therapist Initials
A1. Define Your Experience			
A2. Mapping Your Anxiety Cycle			
A3. Situational, Persistent, Cumulative			
A4. Identify Anxiety Narratives			
A5. Timeline of Resilience			

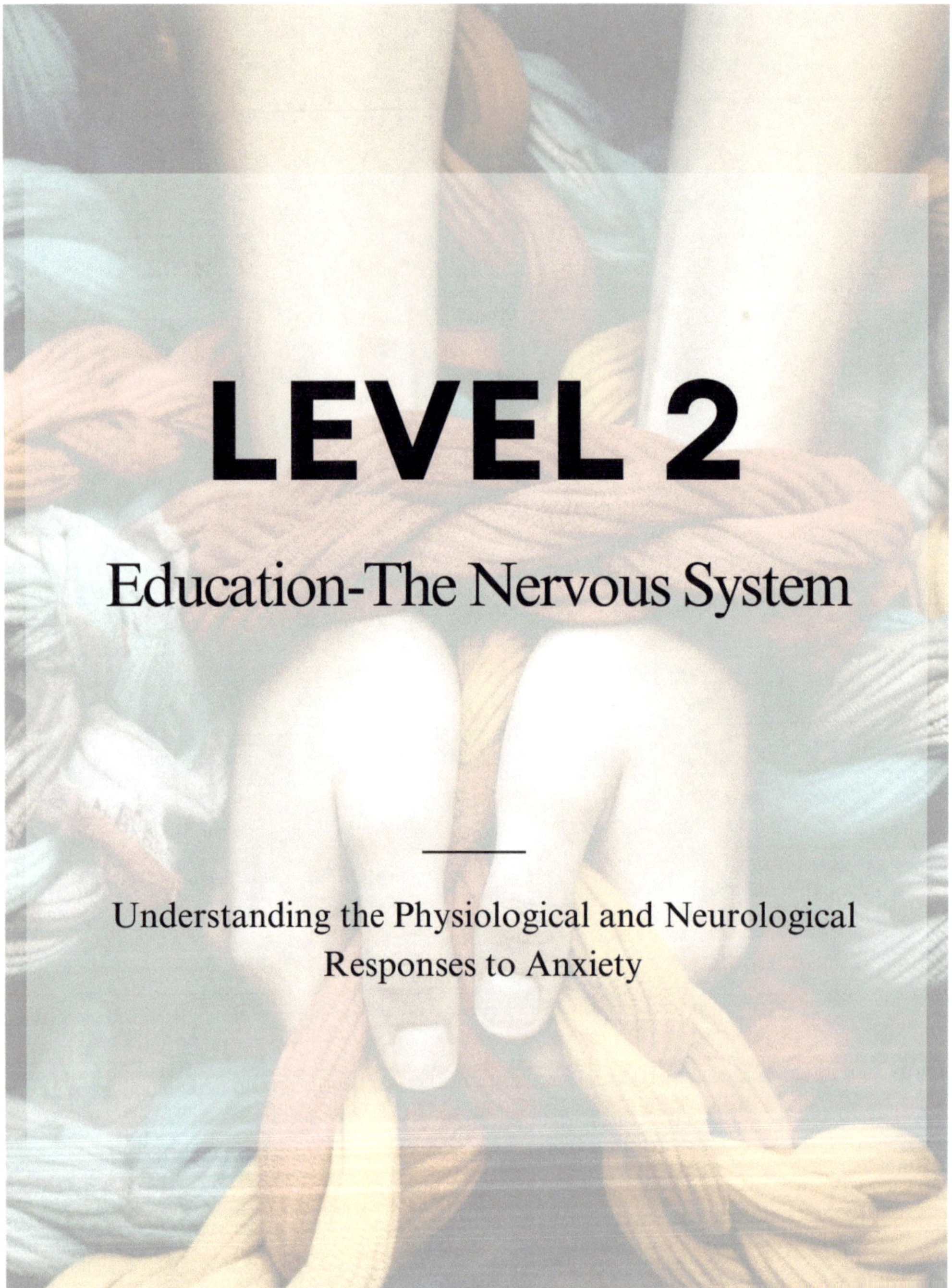

LEVEL 2

Education-The Nervous System

Understanding the Physiological and Neurological Responses to Anxiety

Understanding the Nervous System: The Key to Reclaiming Calm

One of the most important steps in anxiety recovery is learning how your nervous system contributes to—and maintains—your anxious responses. Anxiety isn't just a mental loop of worry; it's a full-body experience. Your brain and body are constantly communicating, and when your nervous system is dysregulated, it can lead to cycles of overthinking, restlessness, tension, or even complete emotional shutdown.

The nervous system is designed to help you respond to threat, but for many individuals living with chronic anxiety, this system becomes overly sensitive—detecting danger even when none is present. The result? You may find yourself living in a near-constant state of fight (irritability, muscle tension), flight (avoidance, agitation), freeze (mental fog, dissociation), or fawn (people-pleasing, self-abandonment). These patterns are not flaws—they are learned physiological habits that can be unlearned.

When you begin to understand how your body responds to stress, something powerful happens: you stop blaming yourself for your reactions and start working with your biology, not against it. You'll learn to notice signs of dysregulation—racing thoughts, shallow breathing, tight muscles—and apply calming, grounding strategies that help restore balance.

Nervous system education is not just interesting—it's essential. Without understanding why your body reacts the way it does, anxiety can feel like a mystery or a personal failure. But when you understand the science, you gain the ability to interrupt the anxiety loop and re-train your system toward calm, clarity, and confidence.

Autonomic Nervous System

Sympathetic Nervous System: Stress Response

Fight or Flight

- Prepares body for stress
- Cortisol and adrenaline
- Increases heart rate and blood pressure
- Decreases digestion

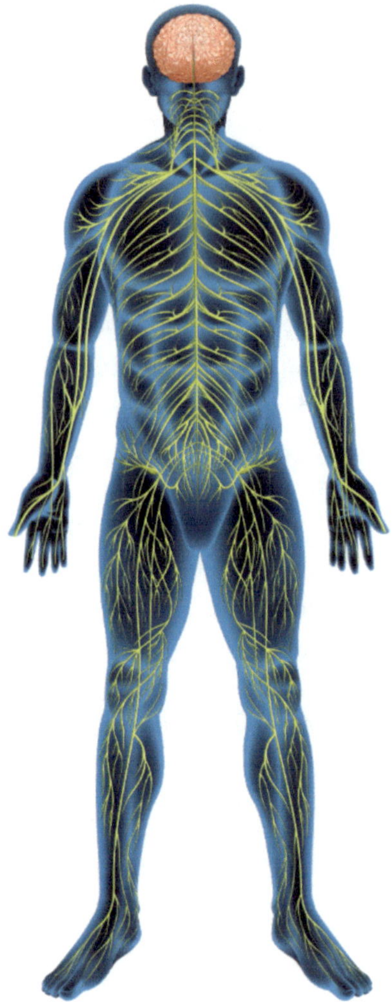

Parasympathetic Nervous System: Relaxation Response

Rest and DIgest

- Returns the body to a calm state
- Growth hormones, DHEA, Melatonin
- Decreased heart rate and blood pressure
- Repairs the body

The Role of the Nervous System in Anxiety

Anxiety deeply affects the nervous system, activating stress responses that influence your emotional, cognitive, and physical well-being. Whether sparked by a real challenge or simply a perceived threat, the brain often interprets certain situations as requiring immediate action—even when no danger is present. In response, the autonomic nervous system (ANS) becomes activated.

This reaction is adaptive in the short term, preparing your body to deal with stress. But when anxiety becomes a recurring pattern, the nervous system can remain in an overactivated state, leading to chronic symptoms that disrupt your ability to feel calm, focused, and connected.

Understanding how your nervous system responds to anxiety is an essential part of learning how to regulate it and reclaim a sense of steadiness.

How Anxiety Engages the Nervous System

Sympathetic Nervous System (SNS):

This is your "fight-or-flight" system. It gears the body up to respond to a perceived threat by increasing heart rate, sharpening focus, and releasing stress hormones like adrenaline. In anxiety, this system may be triggered by everyday situations—like receiving a text, making a mistake, or being uncertain—leading to muscle tension, restlessness, digestive issues, and chronic hypervigilance. While helpful in moments of true danger, prolonged SNS activation wears down the body and reinforces anxiety cycles.

Parasympathetic Nervous System (PNS):

Known as the "rest-and-digest" system, the PNS helps counterbalance the stress response by promoting calm, digestion, and recovery. Learning to stimulate the PNS intentionally—through breath work, grounding, or movement—can help deactivate the alarm state and signal to your body that it's safe to slow down. This shift is critical for long-term anxiety recovery.

The Physiological Effects of Anxiety

Anxiety doesn't just stay in your head—it plays out throughout your entire body. Prolonged anxiety can contribute to:

- **Elevated Stress Hormones:** Chronically high levels of cortisol and adrenaline can interfere with sleep, reduce immune function, and increase inflammation, leading to fatigue or burnout.
- **Cognitive Challenges:** It becomes harder to focus, remember details, or stay mentally present when the brain is stuck scanning for threats or rehearsing "what-if" scenarios.
- **Sleep Disruptions:** Difficulty falling or staying asleep, racing thoughts at night, or even anxiety-related dreams are common signs that your system hasn't downshifted into calm.
- **Somatic (Physical) Symptoms:** Chest tightness, gastrointestinal discomfort, headaches, jaw tension, or shallow breathing are all common ways anxiety manifests in the body.

These responses are not "dramatic" or "made up"—they're the body's way of reacting to perceived stress. But when this response becomes habitual, it limits your capacity to rest, recover, and connect. That's why learning to regulate the nervous system is foundational for lasting anxiety recovery.

Understanding Your Anxiety Tolerance: A Temperature Check

Your nervous system is constantly working in the background, much like a thermostat, adjusting your internal state based on how safe or uncertain a situation feels. In anxiety recovery, it's important to become aware of how much distress your system can handle before it either shuts down, ramps up, or checks out. This is called your anxiety tolerance—your personal range of emotional capacity before symptoms become too much to manage.

Imagine this as a temperature scale:

- On the low end, you may feel under-stimulated, disengaged, or numb. For some, this can feel like zoning out, avoiding challenges, or struggling to connect emotionally.
- On the high end, anxiety may feel like racing thoughts, physical tension, irritability, or emotional flooding—what many describe as being "wired and tired" or mentally overloaded.

If your anxiety level is too low, the tools in this workbook may not feel relevant or may be dismissed as unnecessary. If your anxiety is too high, it becomes difficult to absorb or apply new strategies—you may feel scattered, shut down, or stuck in survival mode.

Your goal is to find your optimal zone—a place where your nervous system is activated just enough to stay engaged, but not so much that you become overwhelmed. This is the space where learning, growth, and change happen.

Later in the workbook, you'll use a tool called the SUD scale (Subjective Units of Distress) to help you measure and track your anxiety levels in real time. This will allow you to adjust your approach based on where you are in the moment—making your work more effective, and your progress more sustainable.

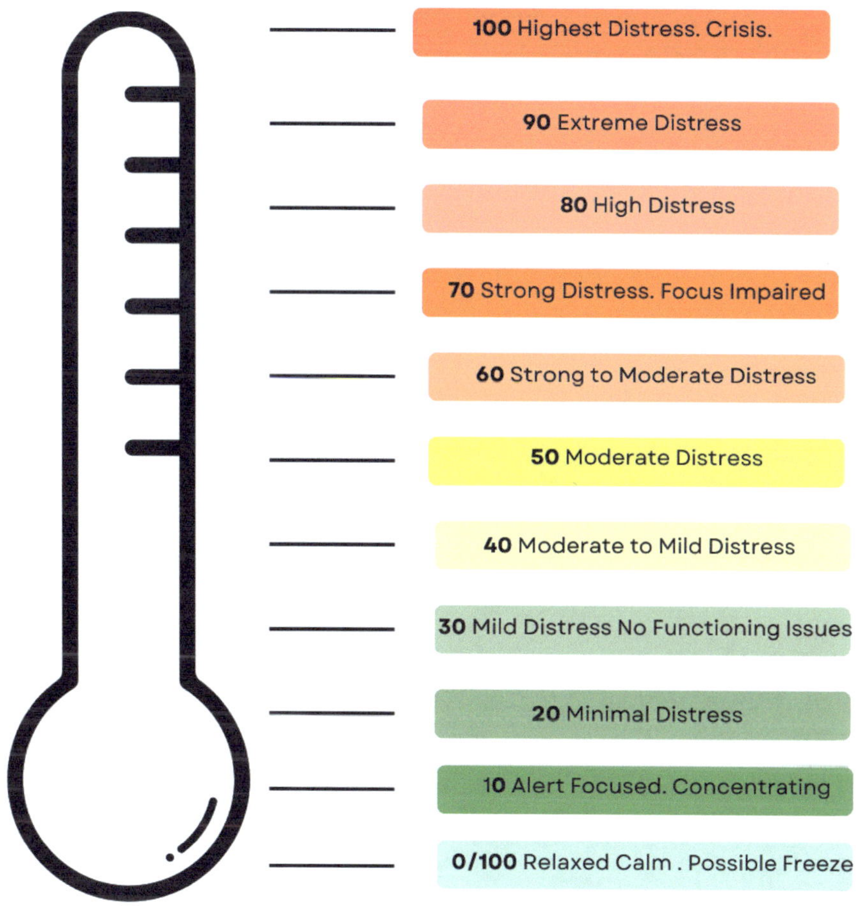
100 Highest Distress. Crisis.
90 Extreme Distress
80 High Distress
70 Strong Distress. Focus Impaired
60 Strong to Moderate Distress
50 Moderate Distress
40 Moderate to Mild Distress
30 Mild Distress No Functioning Issues
20 Minimal Distress
10 Alert Focused. Concentrating
0/100 Relaxed Calm . Possible Freeze

Assignment 1: Finding Your Optimal Zone

Step 1: Visualize Your Distress Thermometer

Think of your nervous system like a thermometer ranging from 0–100. At the low end (0–10), you may feel calm or even disengaged—sometimes this can show up as flatness, boredom, or numbing out. At the high end (90–100), you may feel emotionally flooded, scattered, or at your limit—unable to think clearly or apply helpful tools.

The Anxiety Thermometer graphic included in this workbook breaks down the spectrum from minimal arousal to high distress. Use this visual as a reference throughout your journey to monitor your nervous system activation.

Step 2: Assess Your Current Stress Level

Where would you place yourself on the thermometer *right now*?

- **Low Activation (0–30):** You may feel calm and clear-headed—or disconnected and unmotivated. This might feel like mental fog or low energy.

- **Moderate Activation (30–50):** You're noticing some tension or anxious thoughts, but you remain present, alert, and relatively focused.

- **Optimal Engagement Zone (40–70):** This is the "just right" range—your nervous system is activated enough to support learning, but not so activated that you shut down.

- **High Activation (70–100):** You may feel overwhelmed, agitated, or on edge. Your thinking may become rigid, reactive, or chaotic, making it harder to focus or integrate new skills.

Step 3: Identifying Your Personal Optimal Zone

Your nervous system is unique. Some people learn best around a 50, while others need to stay closer to 30 to remain grounded. The goal is not to aim for a specific number, but to identify the range where you feel alert, emotionally present, and able to engage with challenges without being overwhelmed.

To help identify this range, reflect on questions like:

- When do I feel most focused and capable—even if slightly uncomfortable?
- When do I start to lose clarity, shut down, or spin out?
- What physical or emotional signals tell me I've gone out of my optimal zone?

Step 4: Record Your Findings

Write down where you currently fall on the scale, and any adjustments you plan to make to get into your optimal zone.

- **My current anxiety level is**: ______
- **My personal optimal zone is between**: ______**and** _________
- **To bring myself into my optimal zone, I will try**: ___________________________

Reflection: Tracking Your Activation

Throughout this workbook, you'll see references to the SUD Scale (Subjective Units of Distress)—a simple way to check in with your nervous system before, during, and after exercises. As you build awareness of your internal states, you'll be better able to adjust your pace, apply regulation tools, and maximize your progress.

Note:
Your optimal anxiety zone is personal. This tool isn't meant to measure success or failure—it's a way to help you work with your nervous system, not against it**.** By learning how to track and adjust your internal state, you create space for sustainable change.

Assignment 2: Nervous System Mapping

Understanding how your nervous system responds to anxiety is a crucial step toward lasting emotional regulation. Your body is constantly scanning your environment—internally and externally—for signs of safety or threat. This happens automatically, without conscious input. In the presence of perceived stressors (even minor ones), your nervous system may shift into hyperarousal (fight-or-flight), hypoarousal (shutdown or disconnect), or fluctuate between both.

Anxiety often intensifies this process. When the nervous system becomes overresponsive, everyday experiences—such as uncertainty, conflict, or even performance pressure—can trigger intense emotional and physical reactions. Mapping your nervous system's patterns helps you build awareness, clarity, and intervention strategies that restore balance.

In this assignment, you'll use the Nervous System Mapping Chart provided to track the physical sensations, emotions, and behaviors you experience in three primary states:

- Regulated State (Calm, focused, emotionally present)
- Hyperaroused State (Restless, tense, overactivated)
- Hypoaroused State (Flat, foggy, disconnected)

This is not about eliminating responses but about increasing awareness and gaining more control over how you respond to stress and anxiety. As you complete this assignment, be patient with yourself—this is about learning your body's language so that you can respond with care rather than react out of survival.

By mapping your personal responses, you'll begin to:

- Recognize the early signals that indicate your nervous system is moving out of balance
- Identify situations, thoughts, or patterns that trigger dysregulation
- Clarify which regulation tools are most effective for bringing you back to your optimal range
- Build self-awareness and trust in your body's signals over time

This map will become a practical reference point for our work together. It allows us to create customized coping strategies that match your specific nervous system profile—rather than applying generic techniques that may not work for you.

Nervous System Mapping Chart

1. Use the chart provided to record what each state looks like for you:
    - What do you feel physically and emotionally?
    - What thoughts tend to show up?
    - How do you typically behave or react?
2. Add specific triggers or situations that shift you into each state.
3. Begin brainstorming regulation tools you've used or want to try in each zone.

Nervous System Mapping Chart

Date	**Trigger/ Event**	**Nervous System State** *(Safe, Fight, Flight, Freeze, Fawn)*	**Physical Sensations** *(Heart rate, muscle tension, breathing, etc.)*	**Emotional Response** *(Fear, anger, sadness, numbness, etc.)*	**How You Responded**	**Regulation Strategy Used** (if any)	**Did it help?** (yes/no/explain)

Calming Practices to Support Your Nervous System

Your nervous system is capable of change—and learning how to regulate it is a vital part of anxiety recovery. When anxiety becomes chronic, the body can forget how to return to a calm, balanced state. Through intentional, repeated calming practices, you'll begin retraining your system to respond with greater flexibility and control. In the following pages—and during our sessions—you'll explore and build a set of practical techniques that help soothe your nervous system, reduce anxious activation, and create a steady foundation for long-term emotional resilience.

Calming Practices to Support Anxiety Recovery

The following techniques are designed to support your nervous system and help reduce the intensity of anxious activation. These tools are not about "fixing" anxiety instantly but about teaching your body how to return to a more regulated state. As you work through these strategies, you'll begin to identify which ones are most effective for you.

1. Deep Breathing

Slow, intentional breathing—such as diaphragmatic breathing or box breathing (inhale 4 counts, hold 4, exhale 4, hold 4)—activates the parasympathetic nervous system and signals your body to slow down. This practice helps interrupt anxious spirals and promotes a return to physical calm.

2. Grounding Through the Senses

Grounding techniques bring your attention back to the present moment. The 5-4-3-2-1 method is especially effective for interrupting anxious thoughts. This exercise stabilizes your awareness and reduces mental overstimulation.:

- **5** things you can see
- **4** things you can touch
- **3** things you can hear
- **2** things you can smell
- **1** thing you can taste

3. Gentle Movement

Low-impact physical activity such as walking, stretching, or yoga can help release tension stored in the body and boost endorphins. These movements offer a nonverbal way to regulate the nervous system, especially when anxious energy is high.

4. Progressive Muscle Relaxation (PMR)

This technique involves tensing and then releasing individual muscle groups in a structured sequence. PMR not only reduces physical tension but teaches the nervous system what it feels like to relax. Instructions can be found in the Tools and Resources section.

5. Safe Social Connection

Interacting with people you trust—whether briefly or in deeper conversations—can ease anxiety and restore a sense of safety. Human connection has been shown to lower stress hormones and reinforce emotional stability.

6. Laughter and Moments of Joy

Laughter, humor, or engaging in enjoyable activities—no matter how small—activates your calming systems and provides emotional relief. Even brief moments of joy create space for nervous system reset.

The Boiling Pot: Your Anxiety

Imagine your anxiety is like a rolling pot of spaghetti boiling on the stove.

The heat is up high, and the water is bubbling over—foaming, hissing, splattering across the stovetop, making a mess. It's overwhelming, chaotic, and your instinct is to stop it immediately. So, you rush over and slap the dial all the way off. You want the boiling to stop. You want the mess to end.

And it does. But what are you left with?

Half-cooked pasta sitting in cloudy, lukewarm water. Eventually, it turns to a sticky, clumpy paste—unusable, unpleasant, and completely unsatisfying. You didn't cook the pasta, you just shut everything down.

This is what happens when we try to shut down anxiety without understanding it.

Your anxiety, much like the boiling water, actually serves a purpose. It's the heat that helps cook the pasta. It's the signal that something important might need your attention. But when anxiety reaches a rolling boil and spills over, it becomes unmanageable—and instead of addressing it with intention, we often react by trying to turn it off entirely. We tell ourselves things like, "This is ridiculous," or "Just stop it." But the brain doesn't believe that. It remembers times when anxiety helped you—when it kept you alert, prepared, or focused. It's trying to help, even if the timing is off.

The goal isn't to *turn anxiety off.* The goal is to *turn it down.*

Like lowering the heat on the stove just enough to let the pasta cook gently—so it doesn't boil over, and it doesn't go cold. It simmers. It becomes manageable. And in the end, you're left with something that's been transformed—not wasted.

This is what emotional regulation is. It's not about forcing your brain to stop reacting. It's about learning how to recognize when you're heating up, when you need to turn things down a few notches, and when you can let the process run without fear of overflow.

Anxiety doesn't have to ruin the meal. It just needs a little attention to the dial.

Assignment 3: Building Your Calm Plan

Why a Calm Plan Is So Important

An anxious thought, if left unchecked, can quickly turn into something much larger. Like a snowball rolling downhill, it picks up speed and mass with each rotation—what starts as a single worry can grow into a flood of worst-case scenarios, distorted beliefs, and overwhelming emotions. The longer it rolls, the harder it is to stop.

Before you even realize what's happening, your mind has convinced you that the snowball is real—that the worst *will* happen, that you *can't* cope, or that something is fundamentally wrong. And in that heightened, dysregulated state, it becomes much easier to make irrational or reactive choices: avoiding, over-preparing, lashing out, shutting down, or spiraling further.

This is where your Calm Plan becomes essential.

It's a strategy you prepare in advance—*before* the snowball picks up momentum. Your Calm Plan interrupts the pattern early, helping you slow the roll before the thought becomes overwhelming. It gives your nervous system a way out. It re-engages the rational part of your brain and puts you back in control of your response, not just your reaction.

Anxiety may still show up—but with a plan, you won't have to scramble or guess what to do next. You'll already know.

Your Calm Plan: Tools for Regulation

Later in this workbook, you'll find a list of calming tools and techniques to explore. These are designed to support your nervous system and help you move from dysregulation to a more grounded state. Together in therapy, we'll identify the strategies that feel most effective for you—based on your responses, preferences, and nervous system patterns.

Your Calm Plan becomes your go-to guide when anxiety starts to build. Think of it as a personal instruction manual—one you can follow even when anxiety makes it hard to think clearly.

Calm Plan

Use the chart below to identify common triggers, the regulation techniques that have worked for you in the past, and the expected outcome of using them. You may not always know the exact name of a technique—and that's okay. Simply describe what you did or what helped, even if it felt instinctual at the time. Over time, this chart will help you notice patterns in what's most effective, reinforcing your ability to self-regulate and reduce distress more quickly.

Trigger (What causes distress)	**Calm Technique (What action will you take?)**	**Expected Outcome (How do you want to feel afterward?)**
Example: Feeling overwhelmed in crowded spaces	Deep breathing, focus on an object, step outside for fresh air	More grounded, reduced anxiety, feeling in control

Reflection Questions:

1. Were there any triggers you hadn't noticed before completing this exercise?

2. Which calming techniques work best for you? Are there any that didn't have the intended effect?

3. Do you need to adjust your plan based on real-world experiences?

4. How does having a pre-planned strategy impact your confidence in handling distressing situations?

Moving Forward with Awareness

Understanding how anxiety impacts your nervous system gives you a foundation for meaningful change. By recognizing the body's natural responses—and learning how to respond with regulation instead of reaction—you begin to reclaim control. These strategies aren't quick fixes, but consistent tools that support your system over time. Healing from anxiety requires patience and practice, but with each intentional step, you strengthen your capacity for calm, clarity, and lasting resilience.

Therapist Check In

Activity	Date Completed	Client Initials	Therapist Initials
A1. Optimal Zone			
A2. Nervous System Mapping			
A3. Building Your Calm Plan			

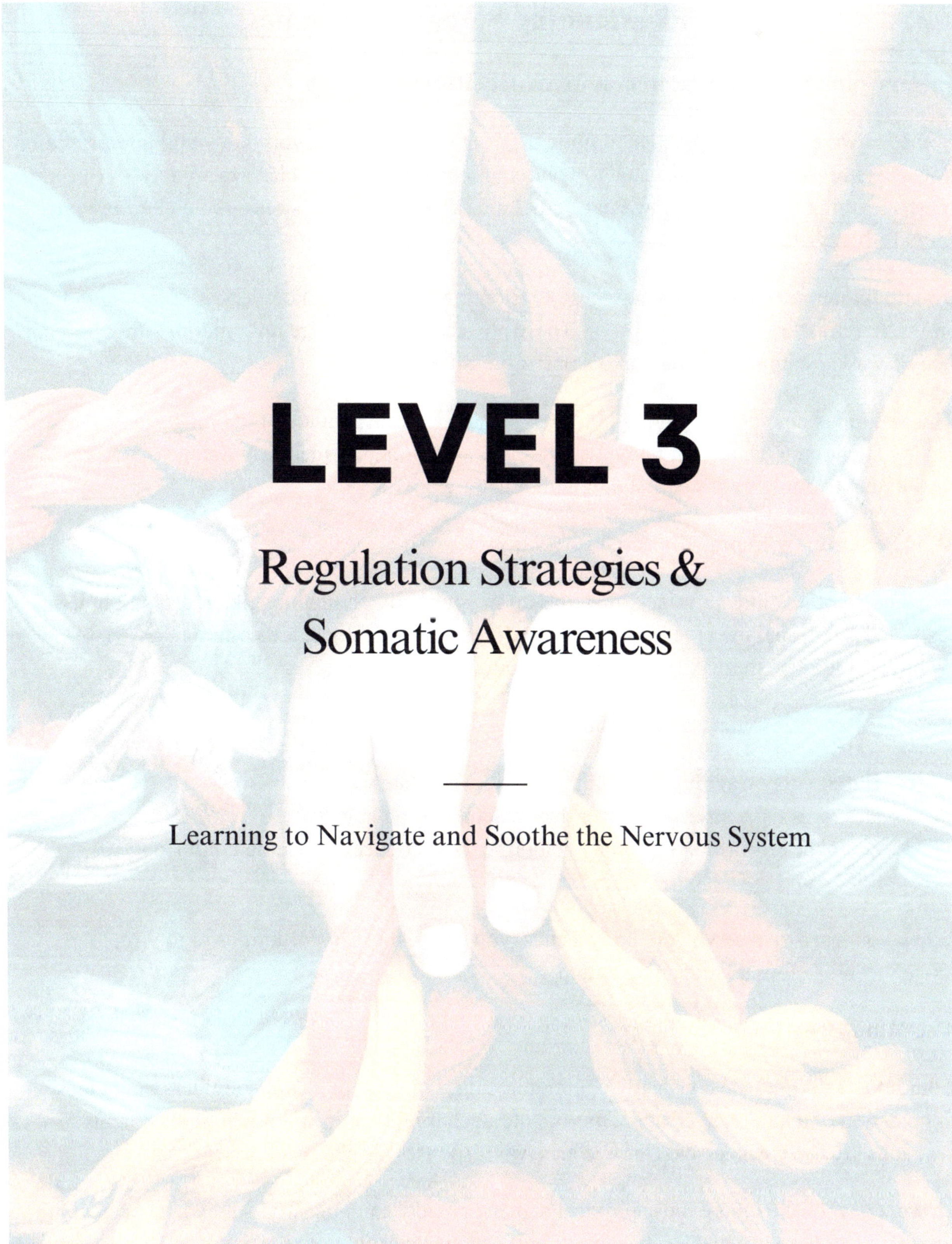

LEVEL 3

Regulation Strategies & Somatic Awareness

Learning to Navigate and Soothe the Nervous System

Understanding Somatic Awareness

Understanding Somatic Awareness in Anxiety Recovery

Somatic awareness is the practice of noticing what's happening in your body and understanding how those sensations are connected to your emotional and mental states. In anxiety recovery, this means learning to recognize how your body holds and responds to stress—often before your mind fully registers it.

You might notice tightness in your chest, tension in your neck or shoulders, a fluttering in your stomach, or restlessness in your limbs. These physical responses are not random—they're your body's way of communicating that it's under pressure.

This section is not about engaging in formal somatic therapy, but about building the skill of paying attention to what your body is telling you—without judgment. By doing so, you can start responding to anxiety cues earlier and with greater clarity.

Why Somatic Awareness Matters in Anxiety

Anxiety is not just in your mind—it shows up in your body. Symptoms like muscle tightness, disrupted sleep, shallow breathing, digestive discomfort, or fatigue are common. Often, we ignore or minimize these signs until they become overwhelming.

Building somatic awareness helps you:

- **Catch early warning signs** before anxiety escalates
- **Respond with intention** rather than reacting automatically
- **Connect physical symptoms** to emotional experiences, reducing confusion and self-blame

When you learn to observe your body's cues, you create more opportunities to interrupt the anxiety cycle before it builds momentum.

The Mind-Body Feedback Loop

Your body and mind are constantly communicating. For example, your shoulders might tense in anticipation of a hard conversation, or your stomach might churn when facing uncertainty. These reactions are not weaknesses—they're survival responses shaped by experience and repetition.

However, when we ignore those physical signals, anxiety can intensify. And when we begin to over-focus or catastrophize every sensation, it can create even more tension.

Somatic awareness invites you to take a different approach—to *listen*, not panic. To *observe*, not avoid. When you become aware of how anxiety shows up physically, you can pair that insight with regulation strategies to shift your experience—one breath, stretch, or posture adjustment at a time.

The Science of Dual Awareness

What you're developing through somatic awareness is known in psychology as dual awareness—the ability to observe your internal experience (such as body sensations, emotions, or thoughts) while remaining anchored in the present moment. From a neuroscience perspective, this process engages both the limbic system (which governs emotional and survival responses) and the prefrontal cortex (responsible for conscious thought and regulation). When anxiety is high, the limbic system tends to dominate, leading to heightened bodily sensations and emotional reactivity. But by practicing dual awareness—intentionally noticing these sensations without being consumed by them—you re-activate the prefrontal cortex and restore balance to the nervous system. This not only reduces anxiety in the moment but strengthens your brain's ability to self-regulate over time. In essence, you're training your nervous system to interpret discomfort as information, not emergency.

Body Scan Exercise for Somatic Awareness

This exercise helps you tune into your body with curiosity and calm attention. Anxiety often shows up physically before we're even consciously aware of it. By slowing down and checking in with your body, you begin to build the skill of somatic awareness—noticing physical sensations that may be connected to emotional distress.

There is no "right way" to do this. If certain areas of your body feel uncomfortable or unsafe to focus on, feel free to skip them. This practice is about listening, not forcing. Go at your own pace.

Body Scan Exercise: Checking In With Your Body

Start by sitting or lying in a comfortable position. Gently close your eyes or soften your gaze by looking at a fixed point.

Take one slow, steady breath in…and exhale.

Now begin to bring your attention to your feet. Notice any sensations—warmth, coolness, tingling, heaviness, or tension. You don't need to change anything; just observe. Ask yourself:

> *"Is there any discomfort, pressure, or unease in this area?"*

Slowly shift your attention to your lower legs—the space between your ankles and knees. Tune into your calves and shins. What do you feel here? Tightness, fatigue, numbness?

> *"Is there anything this part of my body is trying to tell me?"*

Now move your awareness to your upper legs—from your knees up to your hips. Notice your thighs, hamstrings, and any sensations in your hips or pelvis.

> *"Do I feel any tension, restlessness, or ease in this area?"*

Pause here. Take a slow breath. Let your attention stay with whatever you notice—without judgment.

Continue to move your attention upward, scanning through the body. You may want to focus on the following areas:

- Hips
- Abdomen
- Lower or upper back (or both)
- Arms
- Hands
- Chest (paying attention to your breath)
- Shoulders
- Neck
- Head and jaw

As you move through each area, take your time to notice any sensations—both comfortable and uncomfortable—and observe them without judgment. This practice helps you reconnect with your body and build greater presence in the moment. If you find yourself feeling "caught" or overwhelmed by a particular area, pause. Gently breathe into the sensation, and shift your focus from anxiety to curiosity: *What is my body trying to communicate?* Remember, the goal isn't to fix or force anything—it's simply to listen. And if an area feels unsafe or too intense, you can skip it and return to it later when you feel ready.

Note: Why This Practice Matters

Your body often signals distress before your mind fully registers it. A tight chest, a fluttering stomach, or shallow breathing may seem small—but these are early signs that your nervous system is becoming activated. Practicing somatic awareness helps you catch these signals *before* they escalate into full-blown anxiety.

This exercise trains you to recognize those early "whispers" from your body and respond with intention, rather than reacting out of habit or fear. The more often you practice, the more skilled you become at noticing these cues—and intervening before your system shifts into survival mode.

Over time, this builds confidence and a greater sense of control over both your physical and emotional responses.

Strengthening Your Regulation Toolbox: Applying What Works

As you enter Level 3, it's important to recognize that regulation isn't a one-time solution—it's a consistent practice. What you've learned so far about your nervous system, anxiety patterns, and calming strategies forms the groundwork. You're not starting over—you're building forward.

Now is the time to return to the regulation tools you identified earlier and begin using them more intentionally. Think of this phase as fine-tuning your skills. You've already identified what helps your nervous system find calm—this step is about using those tools consistently and with greater precision. The goal is to develop a personal system you can rely on daily, even when anxiety shows up uninvited. If you're stuck on regulation tools, turn to the Tools and Resources section where you can find more options.

The Vagus Nerve: Your Body's Reset Switch

A key part of regulating anxiety lies in activating your vagus nerve—one of the body's most powerful tools for calming the nervous system. This nerve runs from your brainstem through your chest and abdomen, connecting to major organs like the heart, lungs, and digestive system. Think of it as your body's internal "reset switch"—it tells your system when to shift out of fight-or-flight and return to rest-and-repair.

When functioning well, the vagus nerve helps regulate your heart rate, calm your breathing, support digestion, and ease tension—allowing you to feel grounded and safe. But under chronic stress or persistent anxiety, the vagus nerve can become less responsive. This lowers what's called vagal tone, making it harder for your body to recover from anxious states.

Why This Matters

An underactive vagus nerve can make anxiety feel unrelenting. Without a strong vagal response, even small stressors can keep your nervous system stuck in high alert—leading to racing thoughts, physical tension, and emotional overwhelm. Strengthening this system improves your ability to calm down after stress, enhances emotional resilience, and helps your body return to balance more efficiently.

In the next section, we'll focus on simple, science-backed techniques to activate the vagus nerve and support your ongoing regulation work.

Strengthening the Vagus Nerve: Building Consistency Into Calm

Improving vagal tone is like training a muscle—it requires consistency, repetition, and patience. The vagus nerve doesn't respond to a one-time technique but rather to regular activation through calming practices such as diaphragmatic breathing, humming, cold exposure, or gentle movement. Over time, these activities build your nervous system's capacity to return to calm more easily after stress.

When you strengthen the vagus nerve, you're teaching your body how to shift out of anxious activation and into a regulated state more quickly and effectively. This improves emotional resilience, reduces chronic anxiety symptoms, and builds a deeper sense of control and safety within your own body.

Note: Regulation Takes Repetition

It's common to try a technique and think, *"That didn't work for me."* But vagal activation isn't a quick fix—it's a long-term practice. Like strengthening any other system in the body, it takes time. Your nervous system needs repeated, intentional input to begin forming new regulatory pathways.

Don't be discouraged if you don't feel an immediate shift. Subtle changes—like recovering from stress more quickly, sleeping better, or feeling less reactive—are signs that your system is adapting. Stick with the practices, even when the results feel small. Over time, they build into lasting change.

Vagus Nerve Activation Strategies

Just like the calming techniques introduced in Level 2, these practices are designed to help regulate your nervous system by activating the vagus nerve. By engaging this system regularly, you support your body's ability to return to a state of calm more efficiently. Consider these tools as additions to your existing regulation toolbox:

- **Diaphragmatic (Deep Belly) Breathing:** Slow, intentional breaths that expand your abdomen help stimulate the vagus nerve and shift your body into a relaxed state.
- **Humming or Chanting:** The vibration produced through sound activates the vagus nerve through its connection to your vocal cords.
- **Cold Exposure:** Splashing cold water on your face or briefly using a cold compress on the back of your neck can quickly down-regulate your nervous system.
- **Gargling or Singing Loudly:** These simple, often overlooked actions stimulate the muscles around the vagus nerve, supporting tone and regulation.

- **Gentle Movement:** Practices like yoga, stretching, or slow walking can activate the vagus nerve by reducing muscle tension and supporting breath regulation.
- **Grounded Social Connection:** Engaging with someone you trust in a calm, regulated environment supports vagal activation through co-regulation and emotional safety.

Note: How Often Should I Practice Vagal Activation?

Neuroscience research suggests it takes approximately 15 weeks of consistent practice to build new neural pathways and effectively strengthen vagal tone. At Untangled Mind, we recommend engaging in vagal activation exercises for at least *15 minutes per day*.

This doesn't need to be completed all at once. In fact, breaking it into shorter segments throughout the day often yields better results. Here's a suggested rhythm:

- **Morning:** Begin with a 1–2 minute practice upon waking to set a calm foundation.
- **Midday:** Schedule brief check-ins (2–5 minutes) to re-center during the day.
- **Evening:** End the day with another calming exercise to help your nervous system transition into rest.

These small, intentional moments create a rhythm of regulation, helping your nervous system stay more balanced throughout the day. Over time, this consistency builds resilience, increases emotional flexibility, and reinforces your body's capacity to return to calm more quickly. Remember—change happens through repetition, not intensity.

Autogenic Training: A Self-Guided Approach to Relaxation

Autogenic Training (AT) is a structured, evidence-based relaxation technique developed by psychiatrist Johannes Heinrich Schultz in the early 20th century. It teaches the body to shift into a state of calm by using simple self-suggestions that focus on physical sensations like heaviness, warmth, and steady breathing. Unlike some other practices, AT is not rooted in any spiritual or philosophical systems—making it an accessible and practical tool for calming the nervous system.

AT works by training your mind to send signals of safety and ease to the body. For individuals with anxiety, this can be especially powerful. Through repetition, your nervous system begins to associate these internal cues—like "My arms feel heavy" or "My breathing is slow and steady"—with a regulated state. Over time, this rewires your stress response, making it easier to return to calm after a period of distress.

You might also incorporate gentle imagery to deepen the experience. For example, when focusing on sensations of warmth or heaviness, you might visualize yourself wrapped in a soft, weighted blanket or lying in a sunbeam. These simple associations can increase your body's sense of comfort and security during the exercise.

Note: Initial Responses to Autogenic Training

It's common to feel a bit unsettled when first practicing Autogenic Training. Some people experience racing thoughts, physical restlessness, or even a slight increase in anxiety. This doesn't mean the technique is ineffective—it means your nervous system is adjusting.

For individuals who have spent significant time in a hyper-alert state, relaxation can feel unfamiliar or even unsafe at first. Your body might interpret this shift as vulnerability, which is why some discomfort can arise. These reactions are not a sign that you're doing something wrong—they are a sign that your system is recalibrating.

If AT feels overwhelming, pause and return to a grounding practice you've already found helpful. You can always revisit AT later. The goal is not to force calm but to teach your body, gently and repeatedly, that relaxation is safe and attainable.

Steps for Practicing Autogenic Training

You can perform Autogenic Training in a quiet, comfortable space. Here is a simple, step-by-step guide to practicing AT on your own:

1. **Find a Comfortable Position**
   Sit or lie down in a comfortable position. Choose a space where you won't be disturbed, and allow your body to relax as much as possible.
2. **Start with Deep Breathing**
   Take a few slow, deep breaths to settle into the exercise. Focus on the sensation of air entering and leaving your lungs.
3. **Focus on Heaviness**
   Silently repeat the phrase, "*My legs feel heavy.*"
   - Visualize your legs becoming pleasantly heavy, like they are sinking into the surface beneath you.
   - Take your time with this step, allowing the sensation to spread naturally.
4. **Focus on Warmth**
   Say to yourself, "*My legs are warm.*"
   - Imagine a gentle, comforting warmth radiating through your legs, helping your muscles relax further.
5. **Focus on Heaviness**
   Silently repeat the phrase, "*My arms feel heavy.*"
   - Visualize your arms becoming pleasantly heavy.
   - Take your time with this step, allowing the sensation to spread naturally.
6. **Focus on Warmth**
   Say to yourself, "*My arms are warm.*"
   - Imagine a gentle, comforting warmth radiating through your arms, helping your muscles relax further.
7. **Calm Your Heartbeat**
   Repeat, "*My heartbeat is calm and steady*."
   - Place your attention on the rhythm of your heartbeat. Imagine it slowing down and becoming steady and strong.
8. **Relax Your Breathing**
   Say, "*My breathing is calm and regular*."
   - Notice your breathing becoming slower and more even. Avoid forcing it; instead, allow it to find a natural, relaxed rhythm.
9. **Soften Your Stomach**
   Repeat, "*My stomach is warm and soft.*"
   - Visualize your abdominal muscles relaxing completely, as though warmth is radiating through your core.

10. **Cool Your Forehead**
    Say, "*My forehead is cool and clear.*"
    - Imagine a light, refreshing sensation across your forehead, like a gentle breeze soothing your mind.
11. **End with a Moment of Reflection**
    When you're ready, take a few deep breaths and slowly bring your attention back to the present moment. Stretch gently, if needed, to reorient yourself.

Tips for Success

- **Consistency is Key:** Practice AT daily for about 10-15 minutes to train your body to respond to these self-suggestions effectively.
- **Use a Quiet Space:** Minimize distractions to help you focus during the exercise.
- **Be Patient:** It may take several sessions before you feel the full effects. Give yourself time to adjust to the technique.
- **Avoid Forcing Sensations:** Allow the feelings of heaviness, warmth, and calm to arise naturally rather than trying to force them.

Why Autogenic Training Works for Anxiety Recovery

Autogenic Training supports anxiety recovery by helping the nervous system shift out of the heightened fight-or-flight response and into a calmer, more regulated state. Through repeated practice, it activates the parasympathetic nervous system—the part responsible for rest, digestion, and emotional reset. This shift reduces physical symptoms of anxiety, supports emotional regulation, and builds a greater sense of internal safety and control. By learning to calm your body through simple self-suggestions, you're not just managing stress—you're teaching your nervous system how to recover and build resilience over time.

Trainspotting: Becoming an Observer of Your Anxiety

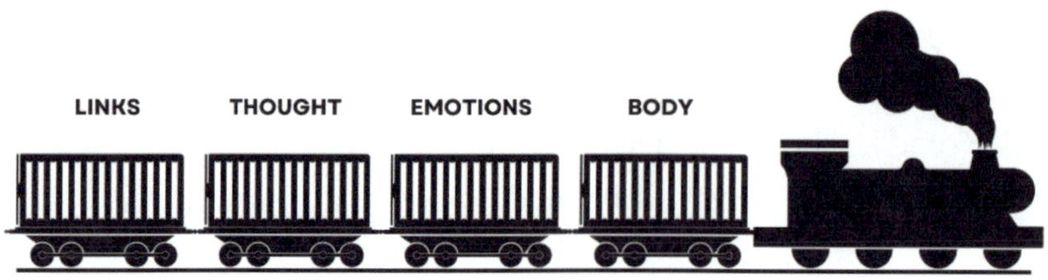

In moments of anxiety, your mind can feel like a runaway train—racing forward with overwhelming thoughts, physical sensations, and emotions all tangled together. You may find yourself "on board," caught up in the chaos and unable to slow it down. Trainspotting is a powerful exercise that uses both bottom-up (body-based) and top-down (cognitive-based) approaches to help regulate the nervous system and bring clarity to your experience.

This technique invites you to step off the train and observe it instead of riding it. You are not the passenger, not the conductor—you are the calm observer, standing beside the tracks, watching each part of the experience go by.

Here's how it works:

1. **Visualize the Train** Imagine your thoughts and sensations as a train speeding down a track. Instead of jumping on, take a mental step back. You are now standing beside the tracks, watching the train go by.

2. **First Train Car: The Body**
   The first train car represents your **body**. Ask yourself:
   What physical sensations are present right now?
   Do a quick body scan—notice areas of tightness, warmth, movement, or stillness. No judgment, just observation.

3. **Second Train Car: The Emotion**
   The next car carries your **emotions**. Pause and ask:
   What am I feeling emotionally in this moment?
   Try to name the emotion clearly. If you're unsure, refer to the Emotions Wheel in the Tools and Resources section to help identify it more accurately.

4. **Third Train Car: The Thought**
   The third car is your **thought**. Ask:
   What thought is connected to this feeling or sensation?
   Try to catch the exact words or storyline your mind is offering—this is the cognitive part of the experience.

5. **Final Train Car: The Link**
   The last car represents the **connection** between the three:
   How is the thought connected to the emotion and the sensation?
   Observing these links helps bring the whole picture together, allowing both your body and brain to make meaning of the experience without being overwhelmed by it.

Assignment 1: Creating Your Regulation Toolbox

Before building your toolbox, refer back to your Nervous System Mapping exercise from Level 2. In that section, you explored how your nervous system reacts to stress and safety cues. Now, we will expand on that knowledge by creating a personalized set of regulation tools to help bring your nervous system back into balance when it becomes dysregulated.

Use this chart to track your experience with different regulation techniques and identify which ones work best for you. Add techniques from Level 2, the vagus nerve activation strategies discussed earlier, and tools introduced in session.

Regulation Strategy	How It Feels Before	How It Feels After	Notes (Helpful? When to Use?)
Box Breathing (4/4/4/4)			
Humming/Singing			
Gargling			
Stretching/Yoga			
Cold Exposure			
Social Connection (Talking/Laughter)			
Autogenic Training			

Regulation Strategy	How It Feels Before	How It Feels After	Notes (Helpful? When to Use?)
Trainspotting			
(Learned in Session)			
(Learned in Session)			

Assignment 2: Self-Assessment –
How Does Anxiety Show Up in Your Body?

Anxiety is not just a mental or emotional experience—it is deeply connected to the body. The nervous system responds to anxious thoughts and environments by activating habitual patterns that often go unnoticed. These physical responses may include muscle tension, headaches, digestive discomfort, fatigue, difficulty sleeping, or a racing heart. Over time, these reactions can become ingrained and serve as early warning signs that your system is out of balance.

This self-assessment will help you observe how anxiety manifests physically throughout your week. By tracking symptoms in real time, you will begin to identify patterns, situational triggers, and how your body communicates stress—even before your conscious mind catches up. The aim is not immediate resolution, but to build body awareness and increase your ability to respond rather than react.

Instructions:

- Use the provided chart to track your physiological symptoms over the course of one week.
  Be specific when noting:
  - **What symptom(s)** you experienced (e.g., stomach tightness, clenched jaw, rapid breathing)
  - **When** they occurred (day/time)
  - **What preceded** the symptom (event, thought, interaction)
  - **What you did** in response (coping strategy, avoidance, self-regulation attempt)
  - **Your distress level** using the SUDs thermometer (0–100)

We'll review your tracking during our sessions to:

- Identify the physical signs your body uses to communicate stress
- Explore regulation tools specific to your patterns
- Develop customized strategies to support recovery and balance

This process will help you strengthen the connection between mind and body, deepen somatic awareness, and take informed, intentional steps toward self-regulation.

Self-Assessment: Tracking Physiological Responses to Anxiety

Date	Time of Day	Symptom Noticed	What Happened Before the Symptom Appeared?	What Did You Do in Response?	How Long Did the Symptom Last?

Reflection Questions

1. **What patterns did you notice in when and how symptoms appeared?**
   (Consider times of day, environments, or emotional states that seemed consistent.)

2. **Were there specific situations, people, or thoughts that seemed to trigger physical distress?**
   (Think about recurring themes, interactions, or thought loops that may have contributed.)

3. **How effective were your responses? Did they provide relief or intensify symptoms?**
   (Evaluate the coping tools you used—what helped, what didn't, and why.)

4. **What adjustments could you make to support your body in moments of distress?**
   (List small, manageable changes that could help regulate your nervous system when symptoms arise.)

Assignment 3: Reflection

At this point in your journey, you've taken meaningful steps to understand anxiety—how it shows up in your thoughts, your body, and your daily life. You've begun practicing tools for regulation and building awareness of what supports your healing. Now is a valuable moment to pause, reflect, and take inventory of your growth so far.

Use the prompts below to guide your reflection. There is no right or wrong way to respond—this is simply an opportunity to connect with your experience, recognize progress, and clarify your intentions as you continue forward.

Reflection on Progress

1. What have I learned about myself over the past few weeks?

2. How has my understanding of anxiety changed since starting this process?

3. What are some of the biggest insights or "aha" moments I have had so far?

Therapeutic Relationship & Self-Exploration

4. How do I feel about my work with my therapist?

    - Do I feel comfortable and supported in my sessions?
    - Have I noticed any patterns in how I engage in therapy?
    - Are there things I wish to bring up or explore further with my therapist?

Tools & Techniques

5. Which tools or exercises have been the most helpful so far?

    - Nervous system regulation techniques (breathing, grounding, movement)?
    - Cognitive tools (thought reframing, identifying anxiety narratives)?
    - Somatic awareness practices (body scans, tracking sensations)?

6. Which strategies have felt challenging, and why?

7. What do I hope to gain in the coming weeks?

8. Are there specific areas of my healing that I want to focus on more deeply?

9. What is one thing I want to remind myself as I continue this work?

Therapist Check In

Activity	Date Completed	Client Initials	Therapist Initials
A1. Creating Your Regultion Toolbox			
A2. Self Assessment: How Does Anxiety Show Up in Your Body?			
A3. Reflection			

LEVEL 4

Attachment & Anxiety

Building Relational Confidence and Emotional Security

Attachment Theory and Anxiety

Attachment theory, developed by John Bowlby, helps explain how our earliest relationships shape the way we experience stress, seek comfort, and manage anxiety throughout life. Our attachment styles—secure, anxious, avoidant, and disorganized—are formed in childhood but often play out well into adulthood, especially when we're under emotional distress.

For many, anxiety doesn't exist in a vacuum. It's tied to relational templates that formed early on—how you learned to get your needs met (or not), how safe you felt expressing vulnerability, and whether reassurance was consistent or conditional. These patterns show up again and again in adult relationships, especially when anxiety is present.

Why Attachment Matters in Anxiety

Attachment isn't just about childhood—it's about how you navigate connection, trust, and emotional regulation in the present. If you felt emotionally supported and safe as a child, you likely developed secure attachment, making it easier to manage anxiety through healthy coping and connection. But if you experienced neglect, inconsistency, or rejection, you may have developed insecure attachment patterns that now show up as hypervigilance, emotional avoidance, or fear of abandonment when stress or anxiety increases.

Anxiety can deepen these patterns. Anxiously attached individuals often experience overwhelming worry in relationships—about being judged, abandoned, or "too much." Avoidantly attached individuals may suppress or rationalize anxious feelings, pushing them down rather than working through them. Disorganized styles can swing between the two, unsure whether to seek help or pull away.

Understanding Attachment Styles in the Context of Anxiety

- **Secure Attachment:**
  You likely have a more balanced response to anxiety, seeking support when needed, trusting your ability to manage distress, and maintaining emotional connection even under stress.
- **Anxious Attachment:**
  You may experience heightened emotional responses to anxiety, a constant need for reassurance, fear of being misunderstood or judged, and difficulty regulating worry when feeling disconnected or uncertain.
- **Avoidant Attachment:**
  You might minimize your anxiety, distance yourself from emotional discomfort, or feel uneasy relying on others. This can lead to internalized stress and difficulty acknowledging emotional needs.

- **Disorganized Attachment:**
  You may oscillate between anxious and avoidant responses—wanting closeness but fearing it at the same time. This can create confusion, emotional volatility, and inconsistent coping strategies in the face of anxiety.

From Awareness to Healing

Understanding your attachment style doesn't mean you're locked into a specific way of functioning—it means you now have the insight to create change. The goal is not to label, but to identify patterns that may be fueling your anxiety so you can work toward healthier, more secure ways of relating to yourself and others.

And this isn't about blaming anyone. Most caregivers did the best they could with what they knew. This is about acknowledging what was missing, what shaped you, and how those early dynamics still influence how you show up today. With this awareness, you can begin to rebuild your sense of safety, trust, and connection—not just with others, but within yourself.

Note: Integrating Your PID-5 Results and Attachment Insights

As you continue to deepen your self-awareness, this is a valuable moment to reflect on how your PID-5 results may intersect with your attachment style. Patterns of emotional and behavioral response—especially under stress—don't happen in isolation. They are often shaped by both your early attachment experiences and your personality traits.

The PID-5 (Personality Inventory for DSM-5) offers insight into how you typically respond to distress, particularly in areas like emotional reactivity, detachment, or impulsivity. When viewed alongside your attachment style—whether secure, anxious, avoidant, or disorganized—these patterns can provide a clearer picture of how anxiety shows up in your daily life.

Using both frameworks together allows us to slow down and examine your reactions with greater clarity. Rather than viewing distress responses as random or unmanageable, we can begin to see them as predictable patterns with understandable roots. This insight gives you more choice—more space between trigger and reaction—and strengthens your ability to respond thoughtfully rather than react automatically.

Refer back to your PID-5 assessments in the Tools and Resources section, and consider how the results reflect your unique style of relating, coping, and regulating emotions.

Assignment 1: Steps Toward Healing

1. **Recognize Attachment Influences:** Reflect on how your attachment patterns shape your response to anxiety. Do you tend to avoid emotional connection, seek reassurance, or fluctuate between the two? How do you currently understand your attachment style, and how might it be influencing your relationships and emotional responses?

2. **How Can You Foster Secure Attachment?**
   Secure attachment provides a foundation for emotional regulation and resilience. What steps can you take to create more secure, trusting relationships—either by deepening current ones or building new ones? What might it look like to communicate more openly, set boundaries, or allow others to support you?

3. **Create Meaning:** Healing from anxiety isn't about eliminating all symptoms—it's about understanding your experience and changing how it influences your daily life. How might you begin to integrate what you've learned about yourself through your anxiety? What personal growth, shifts in perspective, or areas of strength have emerged as you've worked through these challenges?

THE FOUR TRAVELERS

The Four Travelers: A Story of Attachment

The wind howled through the dense forest as four travelers stood at the crossroads, each clutching a worn map with different markings. They had all been walking separate paths, but fate had drawn them together under the sprawling oak tree at the center of the forked roads. The travelers—**Anxious, Avoidant, Disorganized, and Secure**—looked at one another warily, their unspoken histories carried in the tension of their shoulders and the weight of their steps.

Anxious clutched their map tightly, scanning the others' faces, desperate to understand where they stood. "Are we going to stick together?" they asked, their voice laced with worry. "We need a plan—what if we get separated? What if something happens to us?" They stepped closer to Secure, instinctively drawn to the steady presence.

Avoidant stood a few steps away, arms crossed, pretending not to care. "We don't need to stick together," they scoffed. "It's easier to go alone. Relying on people only leads to disappointment." Their map was folded neatly, untouched—because they never trusted it to lead them the right way.

Disorganized lingered at the edges of the group, shifting their weight from foot to foot. "I don't know," they murmured, eyes darting between the others. "I want to stay, but…" They hesitated, gripping the frayed edges of their map. "What if staying is dangerous? What if you all leave anyway?" Their heart pounded with the fear of connection and the fear of isolation, locked in an endless battle.

Secure took a deep breath, surveying the others with calm understanding. Their map was worn but well-read, edges softened from years of experience. "We can walk together for a while," they said, offering a reassuring nod to Anxious, a patient glance toward Avoidant, and a warm but cautious smile at Disorganized. "No one has to go alone if they don't want to."

Anxious exhaled in relief, but their mind still buzzed—what if Secure got tired of them? What if they weren't enough? They stuck close, watching for any signs of distance.

Avoidant rolled their eyes but found themselves hesitating. Was it really better alone? Maybe. Maybe not. "Fine," they muttered. "But if this goes south, don't expect me to stick around."

Disorganized clenched their fists, uncertainty gnawing at them. Their past had taught them that connection meant chaos. What if Secure suddenly turned cold? What if Anxious demanded too much? What if Avoidant abandoned them? Their stomach twisted with the urge to run and the longing to stay.

As the four travelers walked, the forest seemed to shift with them. The road felt more stable when Secure led the way, but Anxious still worried about every twist and turn. Avoidant walked slightly behind, ready to bolt if things got too complicated. Disorganized lingered at the edge of the group, wrestling with their own inner storm.

But as they traveled, something began to change. Secure encouraged Anxious to take deep breaths and trust the journey. "You don't have to prove your worth for people to stay," they reminded them gently.

They gave Avoidant space without pressure, showing them that connection didn't have to mean losing independence.

And with Disorganized, Secure did something no one else had—they stayed. They didn't push. They didn't abandon. They simply walked alongside them, showing them that safety and connection could exist in the same space.

The road ahead was still uncertain, but for the first time, the travelers realized they didn't have to walk it the way they always had.

Understanding Your Deepest Irrational Belief (DIB)

When anxiety shows up in your life, it rarely does so alone. Often hidden beneath the surface of worry, tension, or avoidance is a deeply rooted belief that fuels the cycle—what Dr. Albert Ellis referred to as your Deepest Irrational Belief (DIB). This is the core, usually unconscious, negative belief you hold about yourself—something like "I'm not capable," "I'll mess it up," or "I'm too much." These messages often develop early in life and become reinforced through anxious thoughts and behaviors.

For individuals with anxiety, the DIB is often tied to a need for control, perfection, or certainty. It whispers messages like:

- "If I don't get it exactly right, I'll fail."
- "If I let my guard down, something bad will happen."
- "If I'm anxious, it means I'm weak."

These beliefs are not logical—they're *irrational*—but they feel very real. And the brain, especially when anxious, interprets them as facts. The DIB tends to gain strength over time because anxiety seeks to avoid discomfort, and avoidance gives the DIB room to grow unchecked.

Understanding your DIB is a powerful step in reclaiming control. It allows you to see how anxious thoughts are often rooted in this deep, often unspoken belief about yourself. Once identified, you can begin to challenge it directly.

Take time to consider:

- What fear lies underneath your anxious thoughts?
- What message about yourself seems to repeat across different situations?
- When you're overwhelmed, what belief do you fall back on?

In the next assignment, you'll give form to your DIB. Naming it, personifying it, even sketching it if you choose—these are ways to take the power back. When we bring the DIB out into the open, it becomes something you can challenge, rather than something that defines you.

Assignment 2: Personifying Your Deepest Irrational Belief (DIB)

Your Deepest Irrational Belief (DIB) is that nagging internal voice that feeds your anxiety—the one that tells you you're not doing enough, not being enough, or not safe unless you over-prepare, over-think, or over-control. In this exercise, we take a bold step: we give your DIB a face, a voice, and a name.

By personifying your DIB, you externalize it. You turn it from a hidden driver of anxiety into something you can identify, challenge, and ultimately disarm. This exercise helps you name, notice, and confront the voice behind your anxiety—so you can stop mistaking it for truth. Once the DIB is visible, it becomes manageable. And you are far more capable than it wants you to believe.

1. **Name Your DIB**
   What would you call the voice of your DIB?
   Choose a name that captures its tone, energy, or the way it shows up in your life.

Examples:

- "Penny for Your Thoughts" (always second-guessing)
- "The Commander" (always pushing for perfection)
- "Whispy" (quiet but ever-present anxiety)

   My DIB's Name:

2. **What Does Your DIB Look Like?**
   Bring your DIB to life by imagining its physical characteristics. Use descriptive language—you're painting a psychological portrait.

   - Height/Build: Is it towering and intimidating, small and sneaky, or average and deceptive?
   - Facial Features: Is it stern, mocking, panicked, or blank?
   - Hair/Clothing: What does it wear? Something tattered, rigid, chaotic, or overly polished?
   - Describe Your DIB's Physical Appearance:

3. **What Does Your DIB Cosume?**
   What kind of media, messages, or ideas feed your DIB?
   Does it thrive on fear-based news? Harsh inner dialogue? Unrealistic expectations?

   My DIB is drawn to:

4. **What Does Your DIB's Voice Sound Like?**
   Is the voice in your mind that feeds anxiety booming and urgent? Quiet but unrelenting? Mocking or guilt-inducing?

   - Tone: Harsh, anxious, sarcastic, perfectionistic?

   - Volume: Loud and impossible to ignore, or whispering doubt in the background?

   My DIB sounds like:

5. **What Frustrates You Most About Your DIB?**
   How does your DIB keep you stuck? What does it say that you're tired of hearing?
   This is where you take back power by identifying how it *undermines* you.

   I get frustrated when my DIB…

6. **Give It Form: Place Your DIB into the Human Outline**
   On the next page, you'll find a blank human figure.
   Use it to illustrate your DIB—draw its features, label its voice, and mark where in your body you feel its influence most (chest, jaw, gut, etc.). This drawing isn't about being artistic—it's about giving shape to the formless.

DIB: DEEPEST IRRATIONAL BELIEF

Reflection: Confronting Your DIB

Now that you've given form and voice to your Deepest Irrational Belief (DIB), take a moment to reflect:

- What was it like to name your DIB and give it distinct features?
- How did it feel to view this belief as something separate from your identity?
- What emotions surfaced as you visualized or drew your DIB?

This exercise wasn't meant to be just creative—it's meant to shift your mindset. The act of personifying your DIB helps you separate it from truth. Instead of passively absorbing its message, you begin to *observe* it. You create distance. And in that distance, you gain power.

When your DIB shows up again—and it will—you now have a visual reference. Rather than reacting automatically, you can pause and say:

"I see you, but you don't get to run the show."
"You're a pattern, not a fact."

This is the beginning of disempowering the false narratives anxiety has embedded over time. We will later explore how to reframe and replace these beliefs with healthier, evidence-based thoughts—but for now, the goal is awareness. Awareness is your first defense.

Understanding Attachment Narratives and Reframing Beliefs

Much like the stories told in the *Four Travelers* illustration, we all carry internal narratives shaped by our early relationships. These attachment narratives—formed from how our emotional needs were met or missed—become the scripts we unconsciously follow in adult relationships, especially in moments of stress, fear, or vulnerability.

Cognitive Behavioral Therapy (CBT) teaches us that we can *question* and *change* these narratives. Just because a belief formed in childhood doesn't mean it's accurate or helpful today.

For those with anxious attachment styles, these beliefs might sound like:

- "People always leave."
- "I have to earn love by being perfect."
- "Needing reassurance means I'm weak."

But these aren't truths—they're outdated scripts, often written in childhood. In the next assignment, you'll begin identifying one of your core attachment-related beliefs. You'll explore how it affects your emotions, relationships, and self-image—and start the process of rewriting it.

This is not about erasing the past. It's about choosing what *continues* to shape you and what no longer serves your growth.

Note: "This Is Hokey!"—Or Is It?

You might find yourself rolling your eyes at some of these exercises—especially the ones that ask you to name, draw, or personify something like your DIB. You wouldn't be alone. Many individuals approach these creative exercises with skepticism, thinking, *"This feels silly,"* or *"How is this actually helping?"*

Here's why it matters—and why it works.

When we approach our anxiety only through logic or problem-solving, we engage primarily the left hemisphere of the brain, which governs analytical and verbal reasoning. But anxiety lives in the body, the emotions, and the unconscious—domains more strongly influenced by the right hemisphere, which is responsible for imagery, intuition, and emotional processing.

By choosing creative outlets—like drawing your DIB or writing a personal narrative—you're activating interhemispheric collaboration: the coordinated activity of both brain hemispheres. Research shows this integration strengthens emotional regulation, memory processing, and adaptive problem-solving. In simpler terms: you're helping your brain make more flexible, powerful connections.

So no, it's not just "hokey"—it's neurobiologically sound. These exercises are intentionally designed to access *more* of your brain, not less. And that gives you an edge in managing and eventually rewiring your anxious responses. Give yourself permission to try—even if it feels awkward at first. Growth doesn't always start with comfort. It starts with curiosity.

Assignment 3: Attachment Narrative

Step 1: Identify an Attachment Belief You Hold

Think about a core belief you have about relationships, trust, or emotional connection. This could be something that feels automatic or comes up in moments of stress.

Examples:

- *"If I let someone in, they will leave me."*
- *"I have to take care of others to be loved."*
- *"I can't rely on anyone but myself."*

Write down one belief you've noticed about relationships or emotional safety:

My Core Attachment Belief:

Step 2: Identify Where This Belief Shows Up

Now, consider how this belief affects your life. Does it affect your friendships, romantic relationships, or your view of yourself?

Examples:

- *"I push people away when I feel vulnerable."*
- *"I stay in relationships longer than I should because I fear being alone."*
- *"I avoid conflict because I'm afraid of abandonment."*

How This Belief Affects Me Today:

Step 3: Challenge & Reframe the Belief

Ask yourself:

- Where did I learn this belief? Was it from childhood, past anxiety, or early relationships?
- Is this belief always true? Have there been times when it hasn't played out how I assumed?
- What is a healthier, more balanced way to view relationships and trust?

Examples:

- *Old Belief:* "If I let someone in, they will leave me."
- *New Belief:* "Some people may leave, but others stay. I am capable of forming secure, lasting connections."
- *Old Belief:* "I must care for others to be loved."
- *New Belief:* "I am worthy of love for who I am, not just what I do for others."

My Reframed Belief:

Step 4: Create a New Attachment Intention

To reinforce this shift, write down one small action you can take to practice this new belief in your daily life.

Examples:

- *Expressing a need in a relationship rather than assuming it won't be met.*
- *Notice when you start to withdraw and intentionally stay engaged.*
- *Practicing self-compassion instead of self-blame when relationships feel difficult.*

One Small Step I Can Take:

Reflection Questions:

1. What automatic thoughts or anxieties surfaced as I explored this belief?

2. What parts of this belief feel familiar or hard to let go of?

3. How would I treat someone I care about if they shared this same belief?

4. What could shift in my life if I consistently practiced this new belief?

Assignment 4: Role Play Externalization of Voices

In this exercise, we will use Externalization of Voices. This powerful technique allows you to separate yourself from your attachment-based inner critic and engage in a dialogue with it. Often, our attachment wounds manifest as deeply ingrained beliefs about trust, relationships, and self-worth, and we accept them as absolute truths. However, when we voice these beliefs and challenge them, we can see how they do not define us.

This exercise helps you:

- Recognize how your attachment style influences your self-talk and behaviors.
- Separate your identity from old, unhelpful attachment-based narratives.
- Challenge and reframe limiting beliefs by engaging in a dialogue with them.
- Develop a stronger internal voice that supports self-compassion and secure attachment.

Step 1: Identifying the Voice of Your Attachment Style

Take a moment to reflect on how your attachment style speaks to you. What thoughts come up in relationships or moments of stress? What messages do you hear when you feel vulnerable?

Examples:

- **Anxious Attachment Voice:** *"You have to work extra hard to keep people close, or they'll leave."*
- **Avoidant Attachment Voice:** *"People will always disappoint you, so it's safer to stay distant."*
- **Disorganized Attachment Voice:** *"You want connection but can't trust anyone to truly be there for you."*

Write down one dominant thought that represents your attachment style's voice:

The Voice of My Attachment Style Says:

Step 2: Role-Play – Arguing for the Voice

In this step, you and your therapist will bring this voice to life by engaging in a structured dialogue.

Client's Role: Act as the attachment voice. Fully embody its perspective—why does it believe this thought? How does it justify itself?

Therapist's Role: Argue *for* the voice, reinforcing its reasoning (to strengthen the emotional engagement).

Key Focus: This is not about reinforcing negativity, but rather about *fully externalizing the voice* so it can be examined and challenged.

Step 3: Swapping Roles – Challenging the Voice

Now, you switch roles.

Client's Role: Challenge the attachment voice. *Argue against it—what is flawed in its reasoning? What evidence contradicts it?*
Therapist's Role: Plays the role of the attachment voice, continuing to argue its case.

Examples of Counterarguments the Client Might Develop:

- **Old Thought:** *"If I set boundaries, people will abandon me."*
  - **Reframe:** "Boundaries don't push the right people away; they create healthier relationships."
- **Old Thought:** *"I can't trust anyone to be there for me truly."*
  - **Reframe:** "Some people in my past were unreliable, but I have also had people who showed up."

Step 4: Client Takes Full Ownership of the Counter-Voice

By this stage, you will naturally begin arguing against the attachment voice without prompting.

Final Phase: You fully embody the reframed belief and strengthens your voice.

Key Questions for Reflection:

- How did it feel to externalize the voice?
- What happened when you had to argue against it?
- Did you notice a shift in your perspective?
- How can you apply this awareness to real-life situations?

Reflection and Growth

Anxiety and attachment are intricately linked. The way we relate to ourselves and others is often shaped by early relational experiences, which in turn affect how we respond to stress, uncertainty, and emotional discomfort. Externalizing the critical voices rooted in attachment wounds helps bring clarity to these patterns, giving you the space to respond instead of react.

It's important to remember that an insecure attachment style is not a fixed identity—it is a reflection of learned patterns that can be unlearned. As you engage in reflective practices and begin to nurture more compassionate self-talk, you can shift toward more secure ways of relating—to yourself, to others, and to the challenges that anxiety brings.

Whether your anxiety stems from perfectionism, fear of abandonment, or emotional suppression, the process of identifying and challenging these internal voices allows you to build new narratives rooted in worth, trust, and safety. With practice, these new narratives become internalized, strengthening your resilience and increasing your capacity to navigate future challenges with greater clarity and emotional balance.

Therapist Check In

Activity	Date Completed	Client Initials	Therapist Initials
A1. Steps Toward Healing			
A2. DIB Personafied			
A3. Attachment Narrative			
A4. Role Play: Externalization of Voices			

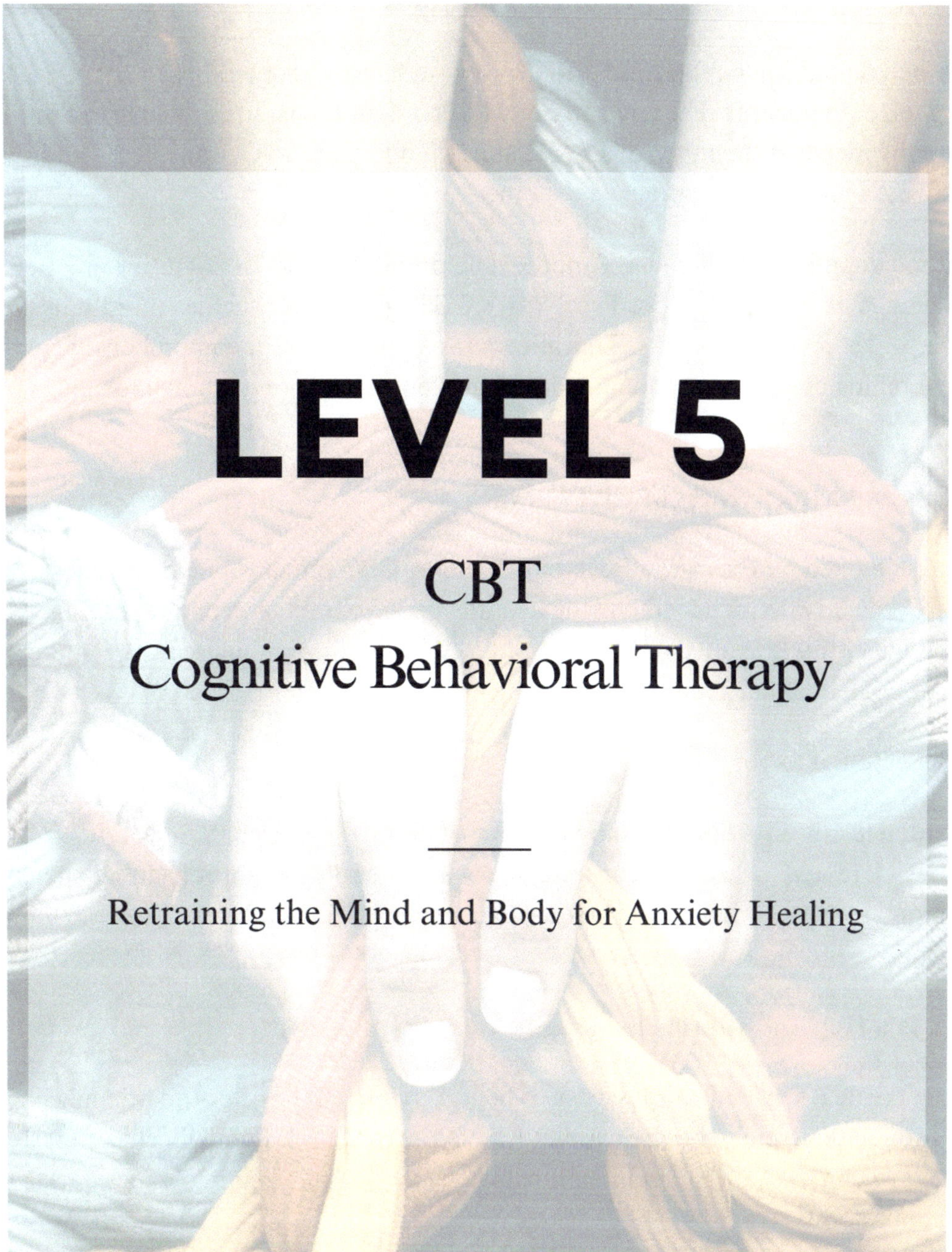

LEVEL 5

CBT
Cognitive Behavioral Therapy

Retraining the Mind and Body for Anxiety Healing

CBT and Why It Works

Working with Thoughts and Behaviors to Address Anxiety

Cognitive Behavioral Therapy (CBT) provides a structured, evidence-based framework for addressing the core patterns that drive anxiety. Rather than focusing on "positive thinking," CBT is rooted in the idea that thoughts, emotions, and behaviors are interconnected—and that by changing one, it's possible to influence the others.

This workbook applies a flexible CBT model, integrating traditional cognitive and behavioral strategies alongside principles from Third Wave CBT approaches such as mindfulness, acceptance, and somatic awareness. This allows for a personalized, comprehensive path to healing that builds on the foundational work of nervous system regulation and attachment awareness.

The Origins and Effectiveness of CBT

Originally developed by Dr. Aaron Beck in the 1960s, CBT remains one of the most well-researched and effective methods for treating anxiety. It focuses on identifying and challenging unhelpful thoughts, reducing avoidance behaviors, and increasing emotional resilience through targeted strategies.

CBT has been found to be:

- **Evidence-Based** – Supported by decades of clinical research.
- **Goal-Oriented** – Provides concrete, measurable strategies for managing anxiety.
- **Empowering** – Emphasizes personal agency and skill-building to promote long-term change.

Why CBT Is a Hopeful Approach

Anxiety can create a sense of helplessness or being "stuck." CBT offers an organized method for breaking through that paralysis. By learning to reframe intrusive thoughts, challenge avoidance patterns, and re-engage with life in intentional ways, individuals begin to experience a sense of control and possibility again.

Branches of CBT for Anxiety

CBT includes a variety of tools and strategies that target different aspects of anxiety recovery:

- **Cognitive Techniques**
  - *Focus:* Identifying and challenging distorted thought patterns, such as catastrophizing, self-blame, or mental filtering.
  - *Goal:* Replace unhelpful beliefs with more accurate and compassionate thinking.
  - *Examples:* Thought records, cognitive restructuring, reframing.

- **Behavioral Techniques**
  - *Focus:* Addressing avoidance, safety behaviors, or overcompensation through structured exposure.
  - *Goal:* Build confidence and reduce fear through repeated, safe engagement.
  - *Examples:* Activity scheduling, graded exposure, behavioral experiments.

- **Third Wave Strategies**
  - *Focus:* Increasing emotional flexibility and distress tolerance through mindfulness and acceptance.
  - *Goal:* Create space between stimulus and response, reducing reactivity.
  - *Examples:* Mindful self-observation, somatic grounding, acceptance-based exercises.

Why CBT Needs a Regulated Foundation

Before the brain can fully engage in cognitive restructuring, the nervous system must be regulated. Anxiety often causes dysregulation, pushing the body into a fight, flight, freeze, or fawn state. In this state, the lower brain—especially the amygdala—dominates, impairing the prefrontal cortex's ability to reason, plan, and reframe.

Grounding techniques, vagal activation, and emotional attunement help bring the nervous system back into balance. Once regulated, the brain is more receptive to the work of CBT—allowing deeper, more sustainable change to take root.

Daily Practice and Consistent Effort

CBT is most effective when applied regularly. Like any new skill, it requires daily repetition and intention. The more frequently CBT strategies are practiced, the stronger the new neural pathways become.

- Skill Application: Use the tools consistently, not just in moments of distress.
- Reflection: Journal and reflect regularly on progress and patterns.
- Commitment: Healing from anxiety is not linear, but persistence leads to long-term gains.

Why the Therapeutic Pyramid Matters

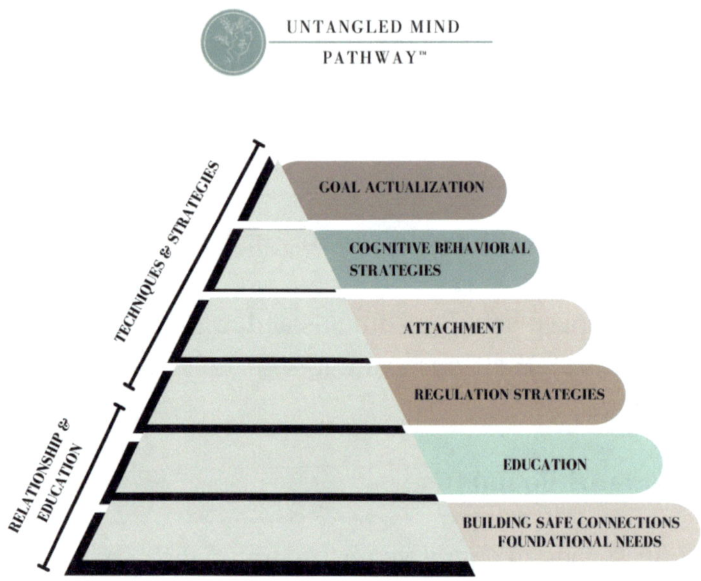

Cognitive Behavioral Therapy (CBT) sits at the top of a therapeutic pyramid. While CBT is a powerful tool for reshaping thoughts and behaviors, its effectiveness relies on a stable foundation. Without nervous system regulation and attachment awareness—the lower layers of the pyramid—CBT may feel superficial or disconnected. When the body is dysregulated or attachment wounds are unacknowledged, the brain struggles to integrate new patterns. By first addressing emotional safety and physiological grounding, CBT becomes a truly transformative method, allowing deeper change to take root and sustain recovery from anxiety.

Cognitive Distortions and Anxiety

When you experience anxiety, your thoughts can become skewed—often in automatic and subtle ways. These patterns, known as *cognitive distortions*, are mental shortcuts your brain uses to interpret information, but they often lead to increased worry, shame, or hopelessness. Identifying and challenging these distortions is a foundational skill in cognitive behavioral therapy (CBT) and a powerful tool in anxiety recovery. Below outlines common distortions, provides examples of how they might show up in anxious thinking, and offers reframed alternatives that promote a more balanced and constructive perspective. This process isn't about "thinking positive"—it's about thinking more clearly and gaining back control from unhelpful thought loops.

- **All-or-Nothing Thinking:** Viewing situations in absolute extremes without recognizing nuance.
    - **Example:** "If I can't stop feeling this fear, I'll never recover."
    - **Reframe:** "Recovery takes time, and moments of fear are part of the process."

- **Overgeneralization:** Drawing sweeping conclusions from a single negative experience.
    - **Example:** "Because this anxietytic event happened, I'll always be unsafe."
    - **Reframe:** "This event was distressing, but I'm working to rebuild a sense of safety."

- **Mental Filtering:** Focusing exclusively on the negatives while ignoring the positives.
    - **Example:** "Nothing I've done has helped me move forward."
    - **Reframe:** "Some days are harder, but I've made progress in small but meaningful ways."

- **Disqualifying the Positive:** Dismissing achievements or positive experiences as unimportant.
    - **Example:** "It doesn't matter that I tried grounding exercises; I'm still overwhelmed."
    - **Reframe:** "Using grounding exercises is a step toward managing my emotions better."

- **Jumping to Conclusions:** Assuming a negative outcome or others' judgments without evidence.
    - **Mind Reading:** Believing you know what others think.
        - **Example:** "They think I'm weak because I'm still struggling."
        - **Reframe:** "I can't know what others think, but I know I'm working hard to heal."
    - **Fortune Telling:** Predicting the worst outcome.
        - **Example:** "I'll never feel safe or happy again."
        - **Reframe:** "I can't predict the future, but I'm taking steps to create a better one."

- **Catastrophizing:** Exaggerating the significance or impact of an event.
    - **Example:** "If I can't stop these intrusive memories, my life will fall apart."
    - **Reframe:** "Intrusive memories are difficult, but I'm learning ways to manage them."

- **Magnification and Minimization:** Amplifying problems or downplaying achievements.
    - **Example (Magnification):** "The way I reacted proves I'm broken."
    - **Reframe:** "My reaction shows I'm human and processing something overwhelming."
    - **Example (Minimization):** "Getting through today doesn't matter; it's not enough."
    - **Reframe:** "Every step forward, no matter how small, matters."

- **Emotional Reasoning:** Believing that feelings define reality.
    - **Example:** "I feel like I'll never recover, so I won't."
    - **Reframe:** "Feelings are temporary and don't define my future."

- **Should Statements:** Placing rigid expectations on yourself or others.
    - **Example:** "I should be over this by now."
    - **Reframe:** "Healing doesn't follow a timeline, and I'm allowed to take the time I need."

- **Labeling:** Attaching a fixed, negative label to yourself or others.
    - **Example:** "I'm weak for not handling this better."
    - **Reframe:** "Struggling doesn't mean weakness; it means I'm human."

- **Personalization:** Taking responsibility for things beyond your control or blaming others entirely.
    - **Example (Self-Blame):** "It's my fault the anxiety happened."
    - **Reframe:** "The responsibility for what happened isn't mine."
    - **Example (Blaming Others):** "They didn't protect me, so it's all their fault."
    - **Reframe:** "I can acknowledge my feelings about others while focusing on my healing."

The Power of Reframing Your Thoughts

Reframing distorted thoughts isn't about dismissing your emotions or pretending everything is fine. It's about interpreting your experiences in ways that are both realistic and compassionate. While the brain can seem reactive and primitive during heightened anxiety, it's also discerning. If a reframe feels exaggerated or untrue, your brain will reject it—and you'll stay stuck in old thinking patterns. That's why this process isn't about applying fluffy affirmations or hollow positivity. Effective reframing is grounded in truth—it acknowledges pain while making room for possibility.

For example:
Distorted Thought: "I should be over this by now."
Reframe: "Healing is a personal journey, and I'm moving forward at my own pace."

This kind of reframe works because it respects your experience while offering a more balanced perspective. The goal is not to force positivity, but to shift your inner dialogue in a way your nervous system and cognitive brain can accept—building trust, clarity, and momentum for growth.

Note: Skip the Affirmation Journals
Please don't tell me you have a positive affirmation journal. Want to see my right temple vein twitch? That's the fastest way. Here's why: affirmations don't work the way social media tells you they do. Your brain is incredibly skilled at detecting nonsense. You can tell yourself, "I am amazing," all day long—but if your subconscious doesn't believe it, it won't stick. In fact, it may increase internal resistance.

We don't use sugary mantras here. We use reframes—realistic, grounded alternatives that your brain can actually accept. That's what creates change. So stop wasting your money on pop-psychology influencers and their shiny notebooks. They don't know your brain nor how it works. We do.

Assignment 1: Identifying Your Cognitive Distortions

Cognitive distortions are exaggerated or inaccurate thought patterns that influence how you interpret situations, yourself, and others. Anxiety often fuels these distortions, reinforcing negative self-beliefs, fear-based predictions, and patterns of avoidance or overreaction.

The goal of this exercise is simple:

- Identify the distortions that show up most often for you
- Understand how they impact your emotional and behavioral responses
- Begin to build awareness so you can challenge them with more balanced thinking

You'll use the Cognitive Distortions on the previous pages as a reference. Start by reflecting on recent moments when your anxiety spiked. What were you thinking? How did those thoughts affect your feelings or actions? Then, match those thoughts with the distortions listed

Step 1: Recognizing Common Cognitive Distortions

From the list of common cognitive distortions, read through each and underline any that resonate with you.

Step 2: Identifying Your Cognitive Distortions

Now, think about some of the negative thoughts you've had related to your anxiety or life challenges. Write them below and identify which distortion(s) they fall under.

Example:

- **Negative Thought:** "If I struggle with my healing, that means I'll never be okay."
- **Cognitive Distortion(s):** All-or-Nothing Thinking, Fortune Telling
- **Rate the Intensity/Belief in Thought:** On a scale of 0-100 how intense if your negative thought, how believable does it feel in the moment.
  Example from above *"9, intensely painful and I believe at 90% for myself."*

Negative Thought	Cognitive Distortion	Rate of Intensity

Step 3: Challenging Distorted Thoughts

For each thought you identified above, challenge it by using a more balanced perspective. Ask yourself:

- Is there evidence that this thought is 100% true?
- Have there been times when the opposite was true?
- What would I say to a friend who had this thought?
- What is a more balanced, realistic way to think about this?

Example Thought Challenge:

- **Original Thought:** "If I struggle with my healing, that means I'll never be okay."
- **Reframed Thought:** "Struggling is part of healing. I've already made progress, and setbacks don't erase that."

- **Rate the Intensity/Belief in Reframed Thought**

Negative Thought	Reframed Thought	Rate of Intensity

Step 4: Reflection Questions

1. Which cognitive distortions show up most often in your daily thoughts? Are there certain patterns that repeat during moments of anxiety or stress?

2. In what ways have these distortions shaped how you view yourself, your relationships, or the world around you?| Consider how these patterns influence your assumptions, behaviors, or trust in others.

3. What emotional responses arise when you begin to question or challenge these thoughts? Do you feel discomfort, resistance, relief, or something else?

4. How could shifting these thought patterns—realistically and compassionately—open the door for progress in your healing? What becomes possible when the distortion no longer runs the narrative?

Thought Reframing & The ABC Model – Breaking Free from Cognitive Distortions

The way we interpret stress, uncertainty, or internal discomfort directly shapes our emotional and behavioral responses. In anxiety, the brain often defaults to protective thought patterns —what-ifs, worst-case scenarios, rigid expectations—all in an effort to anticipate and avoid threat. Over time, these automatic thoughts can become distorted and deeply entrenched, reinforcing cycles of fear, self-doubt, and emotional reactivity.

Thought reframing is one of the most effective ways to interrupt these patterns. Using the ABC Model—a foundational CBT tool—you'll learn how to identify the link between your beliefs and your emotional responses. This process helps create distance between the trigger and your reaction, giving you the clarity to respond more intentionally, rather than being pulled into the anxiety loop.

The ABC Model: Understanding the Thought-Emotion-Behavior Connection

The ABC Model (developed by Dr. Albert Ellis) helps us break down the cycle of how we react to events.

A – Activating Event	B – Belief (Thoughts/Interpretation)	C – Consequence (Emotions & Behavior)
The situation that triggers a thought.	The meaning you assign to the event.	The emotional and behavioral response that follows.

Example Without Reframing:

A – Activating Event	B – Belief (Cognitive Distortion)	C – Consequence
You make a small mistake at work.	"I'm so incompetent. Everyone thinks I'm a failure." (All-or-Nothing Thinking, Personalization)	Anxiety, self-doubt, avoiding work tasks.

Example With Thought Reframing:

A – Activating Event	B – Reframed Thought	C – New Consequence
You make a small mistake at work.	"I made a mistake, but that doesn't mean I'm incompetent. I can learn from this."	Mild disappointment but motivation to correct and move forward.

Tying This to Cognitive Distortions

Anxious individuals often develop automatic, distorted thought patterns as a way to make sense of internal discomfort or external stress. While these distortions may feel protective in the moment, they tend to magnify fear, reinforce negative beliefs, and contribute to chronic emotional distress. The ABC Model is a practical framework that helps identify these thought patterns and reshape them into more accurate, balanced interpretations. When applied consistently, it reduces the emotional grip of anxiety and offers a path toward more intentional, grounded responses.

Adding "D" for Disputation: Challenging Cognitive Distortions

The "D" in the ABC model—Disputation—is a critical step in cognitive restructuring. This is where you directly challenge the distorted thought, using logic, evidence, and perspective. Disputation isn't about blindly replacing negative thoughts with positive ones; it's about developing the mental discipline to step back, examine the thought, and ask whether it holds up under scrutiny.

When anxiety drives your thoughts, it's easy to treat every internal reaction as fact. Disputation allows you to slow that process down and ask, *"Is this thought actually true? Or just familiar?"*

Key Strategies to Dispute Negative Thoughts

- **Evidence Check:**
  What actual evidence supports this thought?
  What evidence contradicts it?
  Is this based on facts, assumptions, or past experiences being projected forward?

- **Reality Test:**
  Am I catastrophizing, fortune-telling, or mind-reading?
  What are the odds of this outcome actually happening?

- **Alternative View:**
  What is another way to interpret this situation?
  If someone else were in my shoes, how might they see it?

- **Compassionate Reframe:**
  If a friend said this about themselves, what would I say back?
  How can I apply that same lens to myself?

- **Cost-Benefit Analysis:**
  What does believing this thought do for me?
  Is it keeping me safe—or keeping me stuck?

By consistently practicing this type of disputation, you shift the brain away from fear-based narratives and toward clarity. Over time, this not only weakens anxiety's grip on your mind—it strengthens your sense of agency. Thoughts lose power when they are examined rather than obeyed.

Assignment 2: Using the ABC Model to Reframe Thoughts

Objective:
To identify distorted thoughts, understand their impact, and reframe them to reduce distress and gain control over emotional responses.

Step 1: Identify a Triggering Event (A - Activating Event)

Identify a recent situation that triggered emotional distress, worry, or self-doubt—this might be a conversation, a memory that resurfaced, or even something seemingly small, like feeling overwhelmed in a public place.

My Activating Event:

Step 2: Identify Your Automatic Thought (B - Belief)

Capture the first thought that surfaced in response to the situation—this is typically automatic, negative, and feels undeniably true in the moment.

My Automatic Thought:

Step 3: Identify the Cognitive Distortion

Look at your thought—does it fall into one of the cognitive distortions? If so, name it.

Cognitive Distortion:

Step 4: Examine the Consequence (C - Emotional & Behavioral Response)

How did your thought make you feel? What behaviors followed?

My Emotional & Behavioral Response:

Step 5: Dispute & Reframe the Thought

Ask yourself:

- Is this thought 100% true?
- What evidence contradicts this belief?
- What is a more balanced, helpful way to think about this?

My Reframed Thought:

Step 6: Identify the New Consequence

With your reframe in place, consider:

- How do you feel when you believe this new thought?
- What behavior or response might change as a result?

Now rate how believable the new thought feels on a scale of 1–7 (1 = not at all believable, 7 = completely believable).

If your rating is below a 4, pause and revisit your reframe. A believable reframe should feel grounded and realistic, not like an empty affirmation. Try again using evidence, logic, or a more compassionate lens to find a thought that holds more truth for you.

New Emotional & Behavioral Response:

Reframing Your Story – The Power of Cognitive Restructuring

Why Reframing Your Story Matters

Your anxiety is real. It happened, and nothing in this process is about minimizing that. The way you understand and tell your story shapes your healing. In psychology, we know that the brain constantly adapts through neuroplasticity—the ability to form new neural pathways and connections.

When anxiety occurs, it often leaves behind rigid thought patterns and deeply ingrained beliefs about self-worth, safety, and control. These thought patterns may have helped you survive at one time, but they can also keep you stuck in fear, shame, or helplessness. This process doesn’t ignore what happened. Instead, it helps you understand and rework how the experience lives in your mind, so it no longer controls your present.

Cognitive Restructuring: Rewriting Your Thought Patterns

Cognitive restructuring is a proven therapeutic strategy used to identify, challenge, and shift distorted or unhelpful thoughts. Instead of letting anxiety dictate your internal narrative, this practice helps you examine your beliefs, offer alternative interpretations, and begin to think in ways that support healing.

- It doesn’t erase anxiety—it offers a new lens for understanding it.
- It doesn’t deny pain—it helps you acknowledge your strength and capacity to recover.
- It challenges thought patterns that no longer serve your well-being.

Memory Reconsolidation: How Your Brain Updates Emotional Responses

Neuroscience shows that when we recall an emotionally charged thought, memory, or belief, it becomes temporarily flexible. This creates an opportunity to introduce new, more balanced information—allowing the brain to "update" how the experience is stored and how it affects us.

For anxiety, this means that the thoughts or beliefs that once felt automatic—“I’m not safe,” “I’ll mess this up,” or “I can’t handle this” can be revisited and restructured. This process doesn’t erase the experience, but it can weaken the emotional intensity, helping you respond with greater calm and clarity.

Memory reconsolidation is the brain’s way of learning that old fears don’t have to dictate current reactions. By pairing these thoughts with new insights and self-regulation strategies, you’re telling your brain, *“This is different now. I have tools. I can handle this.”*

Note: Why You'll See Things More Than Once (And Why That's Good)

Throughout this workbook, you'll encounter exercises that feel familiar—revisited, repeated, or slightly adjusted. This isn't accidental or filler. It's strategy. Repetition isn't about redundancy—it's about wiring new pathways in your brain through consistency and variation. That's how real cognitive change happens.

You don't build muscle by lifting a dumbbell once. You build it through repetition, with just enough variation to challenge the system and reinforce strength. The same goes for your thoughts and responses. You'll approach certain patterns—like fear-based thinking, distorted beliefs, or somatic tension—from different angles. Why? Because that's how we make change stick.

This is also where you begin to identify what tools resonate with *you*. Some exercises will feel natural; others may feel off at first. That's part of the process. This isn't about doing things one perfect way—it's about building a toolkit that works for your real life, not just in ideal conditions.

Emotional Readiness Matters

Before you engage in the anxiety story rewriting assignment that follows, pause to check in with your emotional state. This type of cognitive work can bring up deeper emotional material—especially if you're currently doing exposure therapy or actively confronting difficult triggers.

This workbook is structured intentionally, layering nervous system regulation, attachment awareness, and CBT tools to support emotional safety. Still, only *you* know your current window of tolerance. If this next assignment feels like too much, that's not avoidance—it's wise pacing. You can revisit it later, bring it into a session, or discuss it with your clinician if needed.

This work isn't about proving you're tough enough to push through. It's about helping you develop the insight and flexibility to know *when* and *how* to lean in. That's true resilience.

Note: Potential Triggers Ahead

Some of the upcoming assignments may stir up strong emotions or memories. That's not a sign something is wrong—it's a sign you're digging into work that matters. Still, this kind of emotional activation can be intense, especially if your nervous system is already running high.

Approach each exercise with self-awareness and self-compassion. You are not here to push through at all costs. If you feel yourself becoming overwhelmed, pause.

Check your distress level using the temperature check or SUD scale introduced earlier. Then reach for something from your regulation toolbox. Step away if needed. Reset. Then decide if and when to return.

This is your process. You don't have to power through discomfort just to prove progress. Growth happens when safety and challenge are balanced. Go at a pace that respects your nervous system, your past, and your current capacity. And remember—if you're working with a therapist, flag anything that feels too heavy to unpack alone. You're not meant to walk this road without support.

There are tools in the back of this workbook for moments like this. Use them. You're not starting over—you're learning to move forward differently.

Assignment 3: Rewriting Your Anxiety Story

Objective:
To explore a meaningful experience shaped by anxiety—not to erase it, but to retell it through the lens of strength, resilience, and realistic self-compassion.

Step 1: Writing the Initial Story

Think of a situation where anxiety took over—where it shaped your belief about yourself, your safety, or your ability to cope. This could be:

- A moment when you felt overwhelmed or helpless.
- A recurring anxious thought that feels hard to shake.
- A belief that formed in response to anxiety and still lingers today.

Write the story the way your brain tells it now—don't edit, don't reframe, just let it come out.

My Story:

Step 2: Identify the Core Thought or Theme

What is the anxious belief running underneath the story?
This is often a "truth" your anxiety clings to when stress or fear shows up.

Examples:

- "I always fall apart."
- "I can't handle uncertainty."
  "If I don't control everything, it will all go wrong."

The Core Belief in My Story Is:

Step 3: Challenging the Thought

Ask yourself:

- Is this belief always true, or does it just feel true in moments of stress?
- What evidence do I have that contradicts this thought?
- How would I respond if someone I cared about said this about themselves?

Examples:

- If the belief is "I can't cope," recall times when you did—even imperfectly.
- If the belief is "I'm broken," ask whether you've made progress or shown resilience despite challenges.

Evidence That Challenges My Belief:

Step 4: Rewriting the Story Through a New Lens

Now that you've clarified the anxious belief and gathered evidence against it, rewrite your story from a place of greater clarity and strength.
This version should:

- *Acknowledge the anxiety without letting it define you.*
- *Highlight your ability to endure, learn, or grow.*
- *Include a more grounded and compassionate reframe.*

Example – Before:

"My anxiety ruins everything. I panic, I mess up, and people think I'm unstable. I'll never be normal."

Example – After:

"My anxiety makes things harder, but it doesn't make me incapable. I've shown up even when it's uncomfortable. I'm learning to regulate my emotions and set boundaries, and that progress matters—even if I don't always see it in the moment."

Rewriting My Story:

Step 5: Integrating the New Narrative

This isn't just about rewriting a story—it's about reprocessing it.

Read your revised story out loud. As you do, take a moment to check in with your body. Notice any shifts—tension, release, tightness in the chest, or ease in the shoulders. These sensations matter. They reflect how your nervous system is responding to this new, more balanced narrative.

Now ask yourself:

- Does this story feel more empowering?
- Is it more believable than the old one?
- Can I imagine referring back to this version when anxiety strikes again?

Write down one key insight or shift you noticed in this process:

Behavioral Exercises: The "B" in CBT

Behavioral Experiments: Retraining Your Response to Anxiety

You've likely heard the phrase "face your fears," but when it comes to anxiety, the idea can feel daunting. Behavioral experiments in anxiety recovery are about gradually teaching the brain to respond differently to triggers associated with distressing events. These exercises help reshape emotional and physical responses—not by erasing memories or minimizing experiences, but by helping the brain and body understand that challenging triggers can be managed.

Behavioral experiments are foundational to CBT for anxiety. By systematically confronting avoided situations, thoughts, or environments tied to anxious responses, individuals can reduce the intensity of their reactions over time. This process may feel difficult—sometimes worse before it feels better—but it is a critical part of building resilience and reclaiming emotional control.

Note: If currently experiencing significant anxiety symptoms, it's important to discuss any exposure exercises with a therapist. Exposure work can be intense, and support should be in place before starting.

Why Behavioral Exercises Matter in Anxiety Recovery

Avoidance is a common short-term coping mechanism in anxiety, but over time, it tends to reinforce distress and diminish confidence. Behavioral exercises address this pattern by:

- **Rewiring Emotional Responses:** Gradual exposure helps the brain form new neural pathways, reducing automatic fear responses.
- **Breaking the Avoidance Cycle:** Confronting feared situations directly challenges the belief that avoidance is the only safe option.
- **Building Emotional Resilience:** Each exposure strengthens coping capacity and supports adaptive emotional processing.

A behavioral experiment is a structured test of beliefs and predictions in real life. Rather than assuming a feared outcome will occur, individuals engage in an intentional experience to observe what actually happens. Over time, this weakens cognitive distortions, reinforces adaptive coping, and builds emotional flexibility.

For example, if someone avoids social situations due to the belief, "If I go out, I will panic and embarrass myself," a behavioral experiment might involve attending a small gathering for ten minutes and tracking the outcome. Often, the feared result doesn't materialize—or if discomfort occurs, it is more manageable than expected. This process gradually rewires avoidance patterns with real-time evidence of capability.

But First, Feelings Aren't Facts

In Cognitive Behavioral Therapy (CBT), a core concept is this: feelings are not facts. When preparing for behavioral experiments or facing anxiety triggers, intense emotions will often arise. These emotions may feel overwhelming—but they do not always reflect reality. In many cases, they are echoes of past experiences, not indicators of current danger.

For example, imagine you were humiliated in middle school after giving a class presentation—your voice cracked, your face turned red, and your classmates laughed. Fast forward to adulthood: you're now asked to speak in a work meeting. Your chest tightens, palms sweat, and your thoughts start racing: *"I'm going to mess this up. Everyone will think I'm an idiot."*

The fear is real—but the danger is not. Your nervous system is reacting as if you're still in that childhood classroom, not in a professional environment where things are very different. This is what we mean when we say feelings aren't facts: your body and emotions are responding to a memory, not the current moment.

Anxiety often stems from these inaccurately stored emotional memories, where the brain tags harmless present-day events as dangerous based on past distress. This is a function of how the amygdala (the brain's fear center) and the hippocampus (the memory processor) interact. The brain sounds the alarm, even when there's no fire.

That's why behavioral experiments are so powerful. They allow you to *test the emotion against the evidence*. You step into the feared situation—not to prove you're broken, but to challenge the belief that you're not capable. Over time, your brain learns to *update the story*, replacing fear-based assumptions with experience-based evidence.

Using the Emotions Wheel

To support this process, use the Emotions Wheel. People often default to general feelings like "bad," "sad," or "angry." Research shows that naming emotions more specifically (using the outer rings of the wheel) reduces their intensity. Precise emotional labeling helps clarify the internal experience and facilitates more informed behavioral choices.

For instance, instead of identifying a feeling simply as "anxious," naming it as "overwhelmed," "exposed," or "insecure" provides a clearer understanding of the emotional state. This increased clarity allows for more targeted regulation and reflection during behavioral experiments.

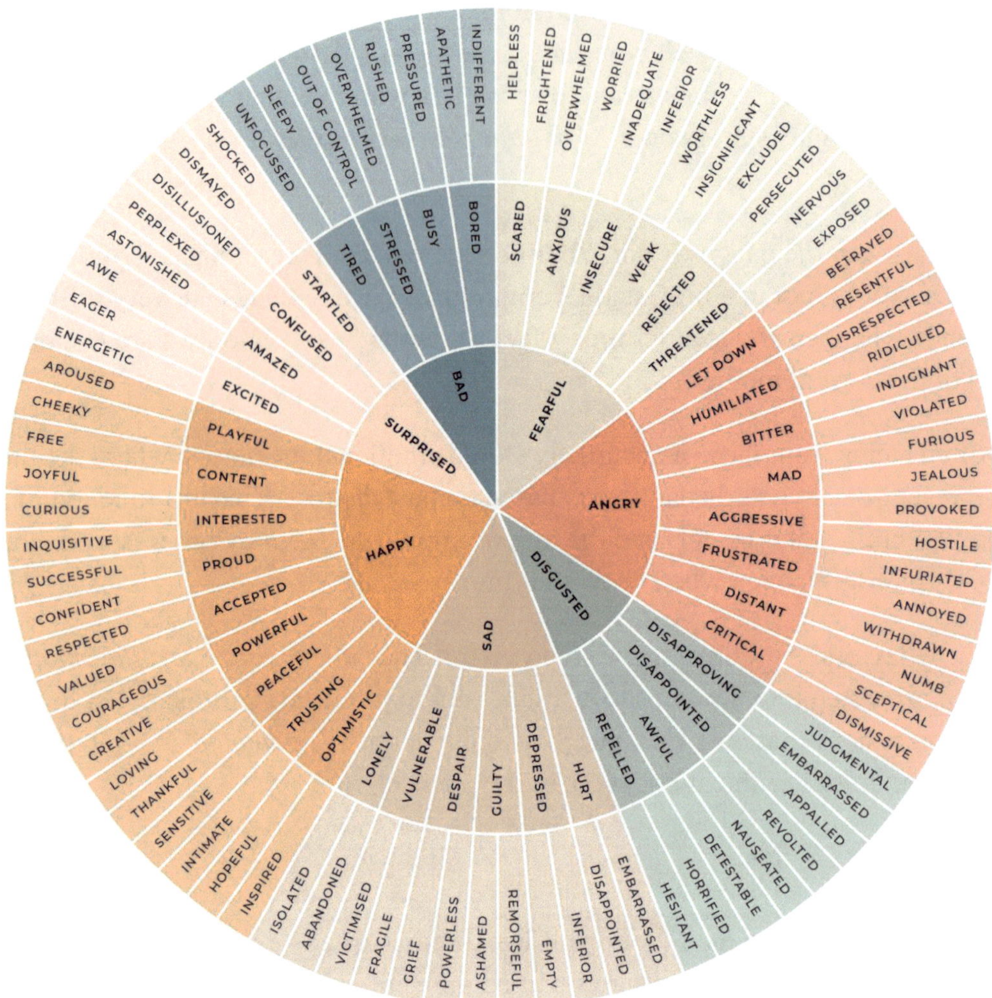
HAPPY
SAD
DISGUSTED
ANGRY
FEARFUL
BAD
SURPRISED
PLAYFUL
CONTENT
INTERESTED
PROUD
ACCEPTED
POWERFUL
PEACEFUL
TRUSTING
OPTIMISTIC
LONELY
VULNERABLE
DESPAIR
GUILTY
DEPRESSED
HURT
REPELLED
AWFUL
DISAPPOINTED
DISAPPROVING
CRITICAL
DISTANT
FRUSTRATED
AGGRESSIVE
MAD
BITTER
HUMILIATED
LET DOWN
THREATENED
REJECTED
WEAK
INSECURE
ANXIOUS
SCARED
BORED
BUSY
STRESSED
TIRED
STARTLED
CONFUSED
AMAZED
EXCITED
AROUSED
CHEEKY
FREE
JOYFUL
CURIOUS
INQUISITIVE
SUCCESSFUL
CONFIDENT
RESPECTED
VALUED
COURAGEOUS
CREATIVE
LOVING
THANKFUL
SENSITIVE
INTIMATE
HOPEFUL
INSPIRED
ISOLATED
ABANDONED
VICTIMISED
FRAGILE
GRIEF
POWERLESS
ASHAMED
REMORSEFUL
EMPTY
INFERIOR
DISAPPOINTED
EMBARRASSED
HESITANT
HORRIFIED
DETESTABLE
NAUSEATED
REVOLTED
APPALLED
EMBARRASSED
JUDGMENTAL
DISMISSIVE
SCEPTICAL
NUMB
WITHDRAWN
ANNOYED
INFURIATED
HOSTILE
PROVOKED
JEALOUS
FURIOUS
VIOLATED
INDIGNANT
RIDICULED
DISRESPECTED
RESENTFUL
BETRAYED
EXPOSED
NERVOUS
PERSECUTED
EXCLUDED
INSIGNIFICANT
WORTHLESS
INFERIOR
INADEQUATE
WORRIED
OVERWHELMED
FRIGHTENED
HELPLESS
INDIFFERENT
APATHETIC
PRESSURED
RUSHED
OVERWHELMED
OUT OF CONTROL
SLEEPY
UNFOCUSSED
SHOCKED
DISMAYED
DISILLUSIONED
PERPLEXED
ASTONISHED
AWE
EAGER
ENERGETIC

Assignment 4: Identifying Your Emotions

Accurately naming emotions is a foundational step in regulating them. Vague labels like *"bad"* or *"anxious"* often don't give us enough information to understand or respond effectively. The Emotions Wheel is a helpful tool for expanding your emotional vocabulary, which in turn supports better cognitive and behavioral decisions.

This exercise will help you move beyond surface-level feelings and into more precise emotional awareness—a skill shown to reduce distress and improve emotional regulation.

Step 1: Start by identifying your current general emotion (e.g., "I feel bad," "I feel off," or "I feel anxious").

Step 2: Use the Emotions Wheel to move outward from the general feeling. Can you narrow it down to something more specific?

For example:

> *"Bad"* might become *"disappointed"* or *"overwhelmed."*
> *"Anxious"* might become *"nervous," "insecure,"* or *"dreadful."*

Step 3: Reflect:

How did identifying a more specific emotion shift your understanding of what's happening internally? Did it give you any new insight into how you're thinking or behaving? What does this emotion need from you right now—attention, compassion, boundaries, or action?

Note:
Like the Trainspotting exercise, using the Emotions Wheel helps shift you from being a *participant* in the emotion to becoming an *observer* of it. This subtle but powerful distinction activates a different part of the brain—one that is more reflective than reactive.

By stepping back and labeling your emotion with precision, you create distance between yourself and the distress. This process lowers immediate emotional reactivity and enhances your ability to respond with intention rather than impulse. Observing the emotion rather than fusing with it is a key step toward emotional regulation and recovery from anxiety-driven patterns.

Creating a Behavioral Experiment

The key to a successful behavioral experiment is to start small and stay intentional. Jumping headfirst into overwhelming situations often backfires—your nervous system registers it as a threat, reinforcing fear rather than challenging it. Instead, progress comes from gradual, well-structured exposure. When done correctly, these experiments retrain your brain by collecting real evidence that challenges the distorted thoughts driving your anxiety.

Rather than diving into a full confrontation with your fears, you'll break the experiment into smaller, tolerable steps that allow you to test predictions and recalibrate your emotional responses. This approach provides clarity, not chaos. It lets you monitor your distress, evaluate the outcomes, and revise your approach—empowering you with practical proof that you're more capable than your anxious mind believes.

Remember, feelings are not facts. By naming the emotion clearly and stepping back into the role of observer (just like in Trainspotting or using the Emotions Wheel), you reduce the intensity of distress. The goal is not to eliminate emotion—but to understand it, work with it, and shift how it influences your behavior. These structured experiments are designed to help you reclaim agency, challenge avoidance, and build emotional resilience one step at a time.

Use the following guide to design your first behavioral experiment. Start where you are—what matters most is that it's intentional, measurable, and grounded in your current capacity. This is your blueprint for change.

The Container: Holding Space for What You're Not Ready to Face—Yet

In neuropsychotherapy, there is a technique often referred to as creating a *Container*—a psychological space where distressing thoughts, fears, or emotions can be set aside until you are ready to confront them. The goal is not to avoid your anxiety, but to create a healthy boundary between you and the material that feels too overwhelming to deal with all at once.

The Container is not about suppression or denial—it's about regulation. You are giving your nervous system a moment to pause while maintaining the intention to return when you're ready. This is particularly helpful when anxiety-related thoughts or avoidance patterns flood your mind, and you need to maintain focus on what matters most in the present moment.

Your container can be imagined or tangible. Some clients create a beautifully designed mental container—perhaps a velvet-lined box, a glass jar with a lock, or a wooden chest placed in a peaceful location in their mind. Others choose to create a real, physical container: a decorative pouch, a repurposed jewelry box, or a customized toolbox. The key is this: make it beautiful and inviting. Make it something you're drawn to, because eventually, you will need to open it—and be willing to take out what's inside.

You might place in your container:

- A fear you aren't yet ready to confront.
- A painful memory that surfaces during an exercise.
- A worry that keeps looping but doesn't need to be solved right now.

By containing it, you aren't avoiding—it's deferred processing with intention. We will revisit your Container in the upcoming section.

Assignment 5: Designing Your Own Behavioral Experiment

To identify an avoidance pattern driven by anxiety, challenge the underlying thought fueling that avoidance, and create a structured behavioral experiment to test your assumptions in a safe, manageable way.

Step 1: Identify the Fear or Avoidance Pattern (Label the emotion)

What situation, place, activity, or interaction do you avoid due to anxiety or distress? Try to be specific.

My Avoidance Pattern:

Step 2: Identify the Thought Behind the Avoidance

What fear-based belief, assumption, or prediction is keeping you from engaging?

My Thought/Belief:

Step 3: Design a Small Behavioral Experiment

Choose one action that allows you to test this belief in real life. Keep the task small and realistic.

- What will you do?
- How will you measure the outcome?
- What's your goal?

My Behavioral Experiment Plan:

Examples:

- *Avoidance Pattern:* Avoiding grocery stores due to fear of panic.
- *Belief:* "If I go, I'll panic and have to leave."
- *Experiment:* Go to the store for one item, stay for 5 minutes.
- *Measurement:* Track SUDs before, during, and after. Did I panic? What helped?

Step 4: Conduct the Experiment & Record the Results

- What happened during the experiment?
- What was your distress level before, during, and after (using the SUDs scale)?
- Did your feared outcome happen?
- What did you learn?

Results & Insights:

Step 5: Adjust & Repeat

- If the fear was disproved, how can you build on this success?
- If it was partially true, what can you learn or modify next time?
- What is your next step?

Next Steps for Growth:

The Role of Exposure Therapy in Anxiety

Exposure therapy is a powerful and evidence-based strategy for treating anxiety. It involves gradually and intentionally facing the specific triggers that cause distress—whether they are thoughts, situations, sensations, or environments. Rather than avoiding what feels uncomfortable, exposure work helps you retrain your brain to respond with less fear, reducing anxiety over time.

The goal of exposure therapy is not to eliminate anxious thoughts or feelings entirely, but to change how you relate to them. Through repeated and controlled exposure, you teach your nervous system that the feared trigger is not inherently dangerous. Over time, this decreases the emotional intensity and physiological response, helping you build resilience and regain a sense of agency.

What Makes Exposure Therapy Effective?

One of the core principles is *habituation*, or the process by which your body and brain become less reactive to a trigger through repeated, low-intensity encounters. The more you face the trigger without avoiding it or escaping, the more your brain learns that the threat it once perceived is either exaggerated or no longer relevant.

Exposure therapy also works by disrupting the cycle of avoidance that fuels anxiety. When we avoid triggers, we unintentionally reinforce the belief that we are not safe or capable. Exposure challenges this belief and replaces it with lived experience—evidence that you can face discomfort and still be okay.

Common Anxiety-Related Triggers for Exposure Work

These triggers vary widely but often fall into these categories:

- **Objects:** Things that provoke anxiety, such as mail, emails, mirrors, or personal devices. For example, someone with social anxiety might avoid checking messages for fear of rejection or judgment.
- **Places:** Locations that spark anticipatory anxiety or past associations, like elevators, classrooms, grocery stores, or waiting rooms.
- **Activities:** Everyday tasks such as making phone calls, attending social events, driving, or even resting—especially if anxiety is tied to perfectionism or a fear of losing control.
- **Sensations:** Physical symptoms like a racing heart, dizziness, or shallow breathing, which can be misinterpreted as signs of danger (e.g., panic attack or illness). Interoceptive exposure—intentionally inducing these sensations in a controlled way—can help rewire that association.

Pacing Is Everything

Exposure therapy must be gradual, intentional, and adaptive to your personal level of distress. Jumping into high-intensity situations too quickly can reinforce fear rather than reduce it. Instead, we build a hierarchy of triggers—from least to most distressing—and progress at a pace that allows you to stay engaged without becoming overwhelmed.

This work is not about "white-knuckling" your way through fear. It's about slowly rebuilding confidence in your ability to face discomfort and remain in control. With repeated exposure, you shift from fear-based avoidance to evidence-based growth—building a more flexible, empowered response to anxiety over time.

THE BIKE

The Bike

The boy was speeding down the street, the wind whipping through his hair, the sound of the tires humming beneath him, a familiar rush of freedom. But then, in the blink of an eye, the bike slipped out from under him. He felt the sharp, jarring pain as he hit the pavement, his knees scraping the rough asphalt. His breath caught in his throat, a gasp of shock and pain. His hands stung as they scraped against the ground, but it was the pain in his knee that made tears spring to his eyes. It wasn't just physical pain—there was something deeper, a gnawing, bitter feeling.

His mother knelt beside him, her hands gentle as they plucked the small pebbles from his knee, one by one. The sting of each stone being removed was a sharp reminder of the fall. His breath came in quick, shallow gasps, not just from the hurt, but from the way his trust in the bike had shattered. The bike that had once been his friend, his companion, his escape from the ordinary world—now it felt like a traitor. It had betrayed him, sending him tumbling to the ground, leaving him bruised, scraped, and angry.

He couldn't understand it. How had something so familiar, so beloved, become a source of fear? He clenched his jaw, resentment bubbling up inside him. He wasn't just angry at the bike. He was angry at himself. "Why didn't I see that coming? Why was I so stupid?" he thought, as the frustration washed over him in waves. He had let his guard down, trusted the bike, and it had let him down.

As his mother soothed him, he tried to quiet the flood of emotions. He sat there, staring at the bike, now lying on its side in the grass like a defeated creature. The sun was bright, but it felt dim. He couldn't shake the image of the crash, the sudden rush of helplessness. The bike had become a symbol of something more than just a ride—it was a reminder of his vulnerability.

Days passed. The bike still sat there in the yard, silent and accusing. At first, the boy couldn't bear to look at it, to even go near it. He steered clear, keeping his distance, convinced that it was waiting to hurt him again. It felt safer to ignore it, pretend it didn't exist.

Then, one morning, curiosity got the best of him. He stood by the bike, looking at it from a distance, his heart racing. The boy took a tentative step forward, inching closer, but his feet felt like they were stuck in mud. He stood there for a long moment, staring at the handlebars, the seat, the wheels that once carried him so freely. His fingers twitched, wanting to touch it, but he hesitated.

Finally, with a deep breath, he slowly picked up the bik and straddled it, his feet still firmly planted on the ground. His pulse quickened, and for a moment, he thought he might back out. But then, something in him shifted. Slowly, cautiously, he lifted one foot to the pedal, leaving the other on the ground. It felt like he was taming a wild animal, his heart thundering in his chest. He stayed like that for a while, his foot grounded, but daring to feel the weight of the bike beneath him. He was still afraid, but there was a spark of something else—a small, quiet resolve.

Each day, he came back to it. Slowly, he placed both feet on the pedals, his legs trembling as he pushed forward, wobbling at first, unsure of himself, but still moving. The bike, once a symbol of betrayal, now felt a little less intimidating. He didn't dare to go fast, but he didn't avoid it anymore either. He was slowly teaching himself that the bike wasn't a threat—it was a tool, a vehicle, and perhaps, just perhaps, a friend once more.

And with each small step, the boy's fear melted just a little. It wasn't about forgetting the pain, but about learning that the crash wasn't the end. He could keep going. And one day, when the fear no longer held him back, he would race down the street again—faster, bolder, and without hesitation—free, just like before.

Creating an Anxiety Exposure Hierarchy

Exposure therapy is a proven method in anxiety recovery. It involves deliberately confronting anxiety-related triggers in a gradual, structured way. These triggers may be physical items, places, situations, or even thoughts that evoke a strong emotional reaction. The purpose is not to erase memories or suppress fear—but to reduce the emotional charge and regain control over how your body and mind respond.

Why the Exposure Hierarchy Works

When you avoid anxiety triggers, you may experience temporary relief—but long term, avoidance reinforces fear and keeps you stuck. Exposure therapy works by gently reintroducing these avoided stimuli and showing the brain that:

- The threat is no longer immediate.
- You can safely engage with the experience.
- You are building tolerance, regulation, and resilience.

Using the Container to Structure Your Work

Earlier, you were introduced to the idea of the Container—a physical or imagined place where you can safely store fears or distressing thoughts until you're ready to face them. Now, we'll use this tool intentionally to support your Exposure Hierarchy.

As you build your hierarchy:

- Write each trigger on a separate slip of paper.
- Assign a **SUDs rating** (Subjective Units of Distress, 0–10) to each one.
- Place each slip into your Container.

Your Container should feel meaningful and safe. You may decorate a real box, journal pouch, or even design a symbolic container in your imagination. The key is that it must feel personal and safe enough for you to willingly take an item out when you're ready to engage.

Assignment 6: Creating and Using an Anxiety Exposure Hierarchy

This exercise guides you through creating your anxiety hierarchy and using it to engage with triggers in a way that reduces their intensity over time.

Step 1: Identify Your Triggers
List situations, places, or objects that evoke strong emotions tied to your anxiety:

1.
2.
3.
4.
5.
6.
7.
8.
9.
10.
11.
12.
13.
14.
15.

Step 2: Assign SUDs Ratings
Rate each trigger from 1(least) to 10 (most) and organize them from least to most distressing.

Step 3: Place Each Trigger in Your Container
Write one per slip with the SUDs rating. Store in your Container.

Step 4: Start Small
Begin with the least distressing trigger. Practice exposure in a controlled, safe environment. Sit with the item for atleast one minute, gradually increase your exposure to the item.

Step 5: Use Regulation Tools
Refer to your regulation toolbox to manage emotional responses during exposure (e.g., grounding, breath work, vagus nerve activation).

Step 6: Reflect and Re-Rate
After each exposure, reflect on what happened. Did the distress level change? Has your understanding shifted? As you continue to expose yourself you will notie that your SUDs lower to the point you no longer feel a reaction to the item.

Step 7: Repeat and Build
As you feel ready, move on to the next trigger in the Container, slowly increasing intensity and tolerance.

Example Exposure Hierarchy

Trigger	Description	SUDs Rating (0–10)
Viewing a related photo	Image of a past anxiety moment	2
Visiting a mildly triggering place	Walking through a location tied to anxiety	4
Making a phone call	Calling someone after fear of conflict	6
Re-engaging in a feared task	Driving, returning to a certain space	8
Talking about the event	Sharing a past fear with a trusted person	10

Reflection Prompts After Each Exposure:

- How did you feel before, during, and after the exposure?
- Did your feared outcome occur?
- What regulation tools did you use?
- What did you learn or notice about your emotional response?
- How would you re-rate the fear now?

Exposure Hierarchy

Trigger	Description	SUDs Rating (0–10)

Why Anxiety Exposure Is Life-Changing

Exposure exercises are not about forcing yourself to "get over it" or pretending your anxiety isn't valid. They're about retraining your brain and body to respond differently to the thoughts, sensations, and situations that currently feel overwhelming. When anxiety builds up over time, your nervous system can begin to treat safe or neutral things as threats. Exposure gives you a chance to break that cycle.

Instead of avoiding what makes you anxious, exposure teaches your nervous system that it *can* handle discomfort—and that anxiety doesn't always mean danger. The goal isn't to erase anxiety but to reduce its power over your daily life.

When anxiety is triggered, your brain may struggle to differentiate between what's truly dangerous and what simply feels intense. Through repeated, intentional exposure, your brain begins to update that alarm system. What once felt like a 10/10 on your distress scale may start to register as a 6… or even a 3. That's not because you've numbed out—it's because your system has learned that it's safe.

Over time, exposure exercises help:

- Rebuild confidence in your ability to tolerate discomfort.
- Loosen the grip of fear-based avoidance patterns.
- Reduce overactivation in the nervous system.
- Give you more choice in how you respond to anxious thoughts and situations.

You won't feel ready for every step all at once—and you don't need to. The key is to go slowly, at your own pace, and use the tools from earlier chapters to support regulation as you grow more capable and confident.

Exposure Practices: Different Approaches

There isn't just one way to approach exposure. Anxiety often shows up internally—through thoughts, sensations, and predictions of what *might* happen. That's why exposure exercises are designed to meet you where you are. Below are some approaches used to help the brain recalibrate its response to perceived threats:

Imaginal Exposure:
This technique involves deliberately visualizing an anxiety-provoking situation in detail. By repeatedly bringing the feared scenario to mind in a controlled way, the brain learns to reduce the emotional charge attached to it. This is especially helpful when the fear is tied to imagined "what ifs," internal dialogue, or anticipated events that haven't actually happened.

Prolonged Exposure:
This involves revisiting an anxiety-related memory or fear repeatedly in a structured, safe context. Over time, the emotional intensity decreases as your brain and body learn that the fear doesn't need to remain heightened. This isn't about reliving pain—it's about staying present long enough to allow your nervous system to reset.

In Vivo Exposure:
In vivo means "in life." This type of exposure involves directly confronting real-world situations or objects that you've been avoiding due to anxiety. This might be attending a social event, driving on a highway, or walking into a crowded store. By entering these situations with preparation and support, you begin to take back control.

EMDR (Eye Movement Desensitization and Reprocessing):
Though not traditional CBT, EMDR is an evidence-based method often used in anxiety treatment. It uses bilateral stimulation (like eye movements or tapping) while recalling a distressing event or belief, helping the brain reprocess the memory in a more adaptive way. This can be especially useful for anxiety rooted in past experiences that continue to feel present.

Reclaiming Your Life Through Cognitive and Behavioral Work

Cognitive and behavioral tools aren't just theoretical—they're practical, strategic ways to take back control from anxiety. Each step you take, whether it's revisiting a location, making a phone call you've been avoiding, or gently confronting a memory, chips away at anxiety's grip and builds your emotional resilience. These experiments aren't about erasing the past or pretending anxiety never existed. They're about shifting your relationship with it.

The "B" in CBT helps retrain the body and brain to stop avoiding and start engaging. The "C" helps you recognize that the thoughts looping in your mind aren't always rooted in truth. When left unchallenged, fear-based narratives and distortions quietly shape your behaviors, your decisions, and your self-concept. But when you confront those thoughts—when you dispute, reframe, and replace them with grounded, truth-based alternatives—you begin to regain your agency.

Behavioral experiments give you evidence. Cognitive work gives you insight. Together, they allow you to live more intentionally, not reactively. The goal is not perfection or fearlessness—it's flexibility, clarity, and the ability to choose your next step from a place of self-awareness, not fear.

Therapist Check In

Activity	Date Completed	Client Initials	Therapist Initials
A1. Identifying Your Cognitive Distortions			
A2. ABC Model			
A3. Rewriting Your Anxiety Story			
A4. Identifying Your Emotions			
A5. Designing Your Own Behavioral Experiment			
A6. Creating and Using an Exposure Hierarchy			

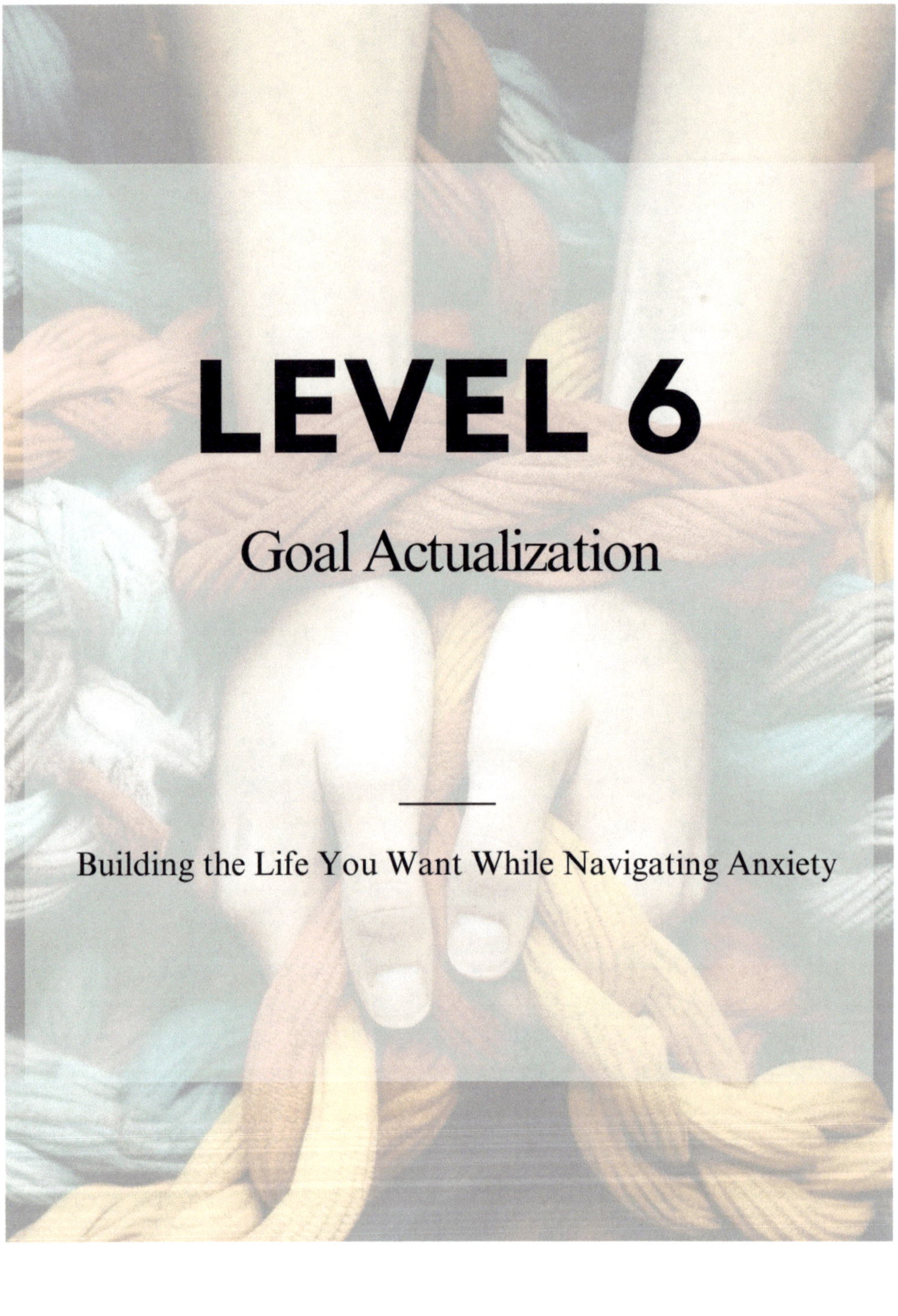

LEVEL 6

Goal Actualization

Building the Life You Want While Navigating Anxiety

Reaching Goals

Resilience, Renewal, and the Road Ahead

Healing from anxiety is not just about managing symptoms—it's about reclaiming your life. Anxiety often narrows your world, convincing you that safety lies in shrinking back, avoiding risk, or anticipating failure. But recovery isn't about staying small. It's about resilience—the ability to adapt, push forward, and live with clarity and purpose, even when discomfort remains.

This level is about rebuilding a future that isn't dictated by anxiety. You've laid the groundwork: regulating your nervous system, understanding your attachment patterns, challenging distorted thoughts, and experimenting with new behaviors. Now, the focus shifts to applying those skills intentionally—to set goals, navigate setbacks, and maintain forward movement.

Why This Final Level Matters

Barriers – Identifying What Holds You Back

Even after doing deep work, internal resistance and external stressors will show up. That's not failure—it's reality. The task now is to notice where you're feeling stuck or hesitant and respond strategically rather than reflexively. Anxiety recovery is rarely a straight line, and recognizing barriers is part of sustaining long-term change.

Compassion – The Antidote to Shame

Anxiety often leaves behind self-doubt and harsh inner criticism. Compassion isn't a soft suggestion—it's a necessary skill. Treating yourself with fairness and patience helps prevent the all-or-nothing thinking that leads people to give up when progress isn't perfect. You're not aiming for perfection. You're aiming for momentum.

From Practice to Persistence

This final level is not about wrapping everything up with a bow. It's about integrating what you've learned so anxiety no longer gets to make your decisions. Resilience means continuing to show up for yourself, even when discomfort lingers. It means knowing that the work doesn't end—but neither does your capacity to grow.

Where you go from here is up to you. Whether you continue therapy, set new personal goals, or revisit these tools during difficult seasons, the foundation you've built is durable. It's there to support your next steps—whatever they may be.

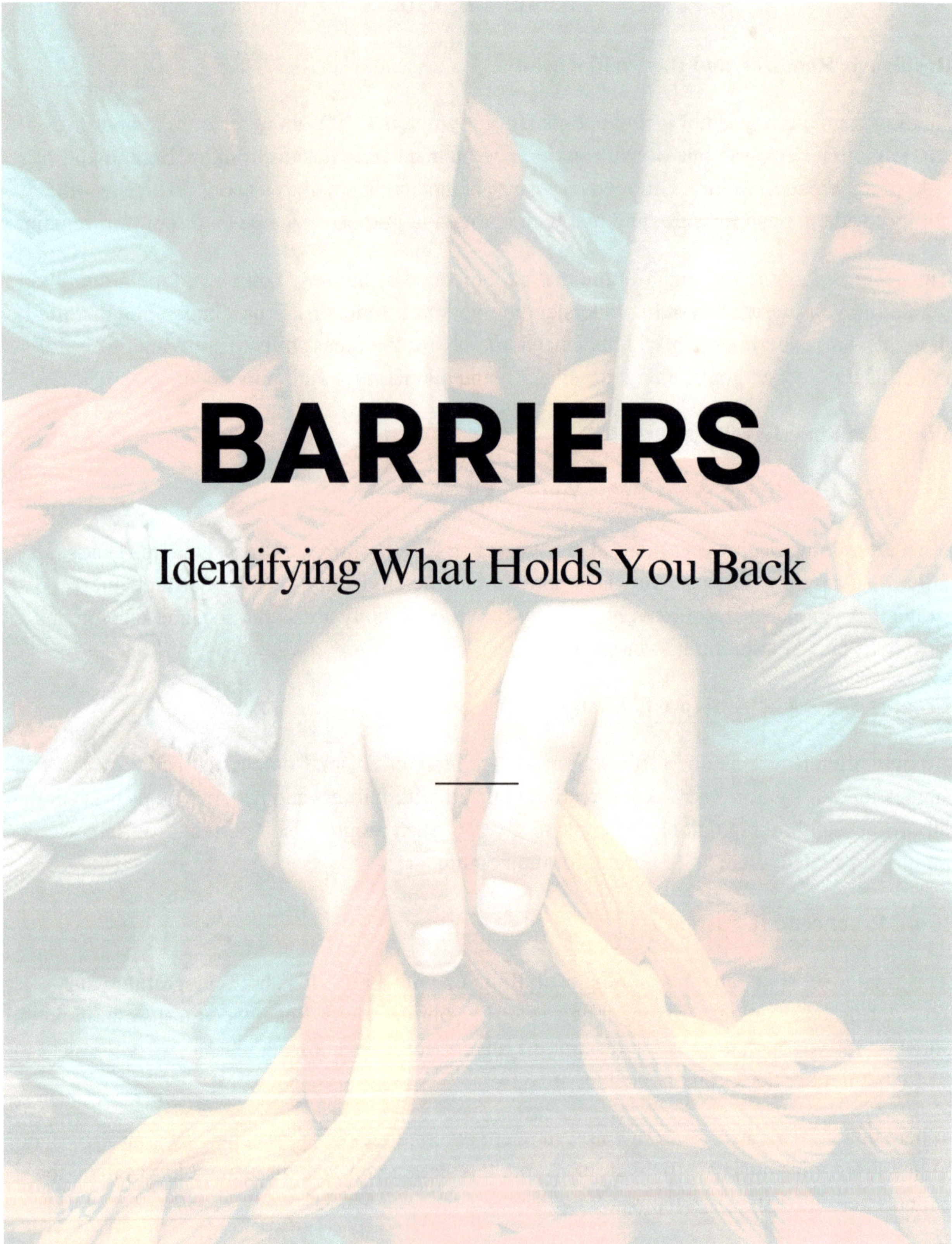

BARRIERS

Identifying What Holds You Back

Potential Barriers to Progress

Recognizing and Addressing Barriers in Anxiety Recovery

Anxiety recovery is not a linear path. As you move through the work of regulation, reframing, and re-engagement with life, it's normal to encounter barriers. These don't mean failure or weakness—they are part of the process. But to move forward, they must be acknowledged and addressed.

Barriers often sound like:

- "I don't have the energy."
- "This isn't working."
- "I can't face that memory."
- "I'll just deal with it later."

These thoughts reflect the brain's protective mechanisms. When you're anxious, your body and mind are wired for survival—not reflection or change. Recognizing these internal and external blocks helps you shift from being at the mercy of your anxiety to actively managing it.

Common Barriers in Anxiety Recovery

Avoidance of Physical Activity
Anxiety can create fatigue, restlessness, or fear of body sensations (like increased heart rate or shortness of breath). But avoiding physical movement only deepens disconnection. The body holds anxiety, and without regular movement to release that energy, symptoms may build: tightness, headaches, or numbness.

Unhealthy Eating or Drinking Habits
Anxiety can affect appetite, leading to over- or undereating. It's also common to use alcohol, sugar, or caffeine as coping tools. While they might offer momentary relief, they can destabilize mood, disrupt sleep, and prolong physiological dysregulation.

Lack of Motivation
When anxiety becomes chronic, it can feel like your drive is gone. Lethargy, indecision, and even fear of progress can keep you frozen. This isn't laziness—it's often a nervous system in a prolonged state of exhaustion.

Doubt in the Process
Many people hit a wall where they wonder, "Is this even working?" This doubt often arises when progress isn't immediate. The work of anxiety recovery is slow and layered but consistent application of tools leads to lasting change, even if it's subtle at first.

The Unspoken Barriers: Risky or Reactive Behaviors

Some barriers don't look like anxiety at all on the surface, but they stem from the same core: an effort to escape. These may provide a momentary sense of relief or control but often sabotage long-term healing.

Sex as a Coping Mechanism
Seeking validation or control through sex is a common but rarely discussed anxiety response—especially when early relationships modeled inconsistency or emotional unavailability. While connection is a core human need, using sexual behavior to numb distress can lead to confusion, shame, or deeper relational wounds.

Gambling and Risk-Seeking
Anxiety can dull your sense of pleasure. The "high" from risk—gambling, spending, even overworking—becomes a temporary escape. But that adrenaline hit masks emotional dysregulation, reinforcing instability and avoidance.

Substance Use
Alcohol or drugs may appear to take the edge off, but they interfere with your body's ability to regulate naturally. What starts as "just something to relax" can escalate into dependency and further disconnect from emotional processing.

Reckless or Self-Sabotaging Behaviors
This might include impulsive spending, confrontational behavior, or even seeking out emotionally unsafe relationships. These actions aren't about "being difficult"—they often reflect an internal state that feels out of control, desperate for grounding, or unsure of worth.

While these behaviors may provide short-term relief or temporary distraction, they perpetuate the cycle of avoidance and prevent true healing from taking place. Understanding why these behaviors are occurring is crucial—often, they are a way to manage or escape emotional pain that feels too overwhelming to confront. However, when left unaddressed, they serve as major barriers to healing.

Why These Barriers Matter

Every barrier—whether physical, emotional, or behavioral—serves as a form of protection. But protection isn't always progress. Barriers like avoidance, risky behaviors, or even unhealthy eating patterns often seem helpful in the moment but ultimately delay healing.

One often overlooked barrier is blame—whether directed inward ("It's all my fault") or outward ("It's their fault I'm like this"). Both forms can stall progress, reinforcing helplessness or defensiveness rather than growth.

The key is not to shame yourself for these responses, but to recognize them. Barriers lose their power when they're brought into the light. As you work through this section, your goal is to notice where you feel stuck—and why—and then apply the tools from this workbook to move forward with intention, not just reaction.

Blame as a Barrier: When Anxiety Gets Projected Outward

One of the most overlooked but deeply embedded barriers to anxiety recovery is the tendency to blame others.

It might sound like:

- "If they hadn't done that, I wouldn't feel this way."
- "My anxiety is because of how they treated me."
- "They're the problem, not me."

And here's the hard truth: sometimes, others *did* contribute to your anxiety—through neglect, criticism, betrayal, or abandonment. But continuing to externalize blame keeps you stuck. It keeps the locus of control outside of you.

Blame can become a defense mechanism. It protects you from painful self-reflection. If someone else is always at fault, then you never have to confront your own thought patterns, beliefs, or behaviors. But what feels protective is actually keeping you in a loop—where anxiety is always happening *to* you instead of being something you can learn to manage from the inside out.

This doesn't mean you excuse the behavior of others. It means you take ownership of what is yours: your response, your healing, and your ability to choose differently.

Why Confronting Blame Matters in Anxiety Recovery

Blame blocks:

- **Accountability** – If the problem is always outside you, then so is the solution.
- **Self-efficacy** – It strips away your sense of agency to change your patterns.
- **Insight** – It prevents you from noticing how anxiety distorts your perception of others.
- **Connection** – It damages relationships by creating chronic defensiveness and emotional distance.

Healing from anxiety requires internal alignment. That means noticing when your mind wants to deflect pain outward, and instead asking:

- "What am I feeling right now that I don't want to deal with?"
- "What fear or insecurity is underneath this anger or resentment?"
- "What part of me is still waiting for someone else to fix this?"

This shift isn't easy. But it's necessary. True growth comes from owning your emotional landscape—even when it would be easier to point the finger elsewhere.

THE KING'S TEST

The King's Test

The kingdom had grown complacent. The once hardworking people had become soft, entitled, and prone to complaint. The king, a wise but weary ruler, had watched this transformation with growing concern. He wanted to remind his people of something they had forgotten—that struggle was not something to fear but something to overcome.

So, he devised a plan.

One evening, under the cover of darkness, he ordered his men to place a massive boulder in the middle of the main road leading into the city. This road was the kingdom's lifeline—merchants used it to bring food, water, and supplies, and travelers passed through on their journeys. By blocking it, the king ensured no one could enter or leave without facing the obstacle.

Then, he hid nearby, watching.

At dawn, the first travelers arrived. A merchant leading a caravan stopped short, his face twisting in frustration. He sighed heavily, turned his cart around, and muttered something about the king's incompetence. A nobleman in fine robes came next, stepping out of his carriage to inspect the obstacle. He tapped the boulder with the tip of his boot, shook his head, and declared, *"Surely, someone else will move this."* Then, he climbed back into his carriage and left.

People arrived one by one, examined the boulder, and walked away. Some grumbled about the inconvenience. Others cursed the king for not keeping the roads clear. A few made weak attempts, placing their hands against the rock and giving a halfhearted shove before sighing in defeat.

Days passed. The king's disappointment grew. Had his people truly lost their will to struggle?

Then, late one afternoon, a lone peasant approached. His clothes were worn, his hands calloused from labor. He carried a heavy sack slung over his shoulder, and as he neared the boulder, he stopped, studying it.

Unlike the others, he didn't turn away.

He set down his sack, took a deep breath, and pushed with all his strength. The rock didn't budge. He pushed again, his muscles straining, his breath coming in short bursts—still, nothing.

He stepped back, wiping sweat from his brow. But instead of giving up, he looked around.

His eyes landed on the nearby trees. A thought sparked. He hurried into the woods and searched for a fallen branch strong enough to serve as a lever. When he found one, he dragged it back to the road and wedged it beneath the rock. Slowly, carefully, he pressed down. The boulder groaned, shifted, then—at last—rolled to the side.

Beneath it lay a small purse filled with gold coins and a note, written in the king's own hand:

"The obstacle in the path becomes the path. Never forget, within every obstacle is an opportunity to improve our condition."

The peasant picked up the purse, turning the words over in his mind. The struggle had been frustrating. It had been difficult. But in the end, it had made him richer in coin and character. And perhaps, that had been the real reward all along.

Adapted fable

Awareness and Addressing Barriers to Recovery

The first step in addressing any barrier—whether it's avoidance, risky behaviors, unhealthy eating or drinking habits, lack of motivation, or doubt in the process—is recognizing it for what it is: a protective strategy that may have once felt helpful, but is now holding you back.

Anxiety has a way of shaping decisions and behaviors without your full awareness. What feels like procrastination or numbing may actually be an attempt to avoid discomfort or fear. Naming the behavior allows you to step into awareness—because what you can't name, you can't change.

In therapy, we will work together to:

- **Identify the barriers** that are actively getting in the way of your recovery.
- **Understand the emotional drivers** behind them—whether it's fear, shame, loneliness, frustration, or self-doubt.
- **Develop healthier strategies** to manage those emotions—through tools like mindfulness, structured journaling, movement, or building daily rhythm and structure.
- **Strengthen support** by identifying people who can offer accountability, encouragement, and grounded feedback.

Recovery isn't just about eliminating behaviors. It's about understanding what need the behavior is trying to meet—and meeting that need in a healthier, more sustainable way.

In the next assignment, you'll name your barriers. This is a critical step. By putting language to what's standing in your way, you begin to take control of the process—on your terms and at your pace.

Assignment 1: Naming Your Barriers

Barriers don't disappear by ignoring them—they fester. Whether external (like time, money, or competing responsibilities) or internal (like fear, doubt, or the belief that change isn't possible), these obstacles can quietly control your choices. But here's the truth: barriers only keep their power when they go unnamed.

This exercise is about calling them out. Write down every reason, excuse, or belief—no matter how small, valid, or repetitive it may seem—that gets in the way of your progress. You're not here to solve them yet. You're here to see them clearly. Because awareness is the first step in reclaiming control.

Instructions:

1. Find a quiet space where you can be honest with yourself.
2. Write down *every* reason, excuse, or obstacle that has kept you from engaging in this healing work.
3. Don't censor yourself; write down anything that comes to mind. Even if it seems insignificant (*"I just don't feel like it"*) or unrelated (*"The cat is out of food"*), put it on the page.
4. Be as detailed as you'd like. If an excuse has a deeper meaning, write it down, too.

My Barriers & Excuses:

Reflection Questions:

1. What themes or patterns do I see across my barriers? Are they tied to fear, avoidance, perfectionism, or something else?

2. Are these obstacles grounded in reality, or are they driven by anxiety-based beliefs I've come to accept as truth?

3. Which of these barriers could shift if I approached them differently or applied tools I've already learned?

4. If someone I cared about faced these same blocks, how would I respond to them? What would I encourage them to do?

Fueling Your Body, Strengthening Your Mind

Healing from anxiety isn't limited to mindset—it's a full-body process. anxiety embeds itself in the nervous system, disrupting sleep, concentration, digestion, and energy. Your body carries the burden of chronic stress, and what you feed it—both nutritionally and physically—can either help calm your system or reinforce its dysregulation.

This isn't about rigid diets or unrealistic fitness goals. It's about intentional care. Consistent nourishment and regular movement help regulate your nervous system, reduce inflammation, and stabilize mood. These choices signal to your brain and body: *I am safe.*

The objective isn't perfection—it's sustainability. When you choose foods that support brain health and engage in movement that restores balance (even just a walk or stretch), you lay the physical foundation needed for emotional recovery. This kind of physical care strengthens the work you're doing in therapy and gives your brain the fuel it needs to stay engaged, resilient, and present.

Did You Grow Up Hearing, "Go Outside and Run Off That Energy?" There's a Reason for That.

Physical movement isn't just for physical health—it's one of the most effective and accessible ways to regulate the nervous system and support anxiety recovery. What your caregivers may not have known is that movement helps release stored survival energy, calm the body, and re-engage the thinking brain.

When anxiety builds, your body enters a state of high alert. That energy has to go somewhere. If it's not discharged through movement, it gets stuck—showing up as tension, racing thoughts, restlessness, or emotional overwhelm. Exercise becomes a powerful way to give that energy a direction and return your system to balance.

Why Physical Activity Matters in Anxiety Recovery

- **Releases Stored Energy:** Anxiety responses like hypervigilance, agitation, or panic are often signs of unprocessed stress energy. Movement discharges that buildup, helping the body recalibrate.
- **Improves Mood and Sleep:** Physical activity stimulates the release of endorphins, serotonin, and dopamine—neurotransmitters that boost mood, regulate anxiety, and improve your sleep cycle.
- **Strengthens the Mind-Body Connection:** Gentle or intentional movement rebuilds trust in your body, reminding you that it can be a source of strength rather than a source of distress.

- **Reduces Physical Tension:** Practices like stretching, yoga, walking, or strength training help loosen chronic muscular tension and reduce the physiological burden of anxiety.

The Role of Nutrition and Alcohol

What you put into your body affects how your nervous system functions—and how well it can recover. It might feel easier in the moment to reach for comfort foods or alcohol to take the edge off, but those choices can work against your long-term healing. Nutrition and substance use aren't just side conversations—they are core parts of anxiety recovery.

Nutrition Tips That Support Anxiety Recovery

- **Eat Balanced, Intentional Meals:** Prioritize whole foods—lean proteins, healthy fats, complex carbohydrates, and fiber-rich vegetables—to support brain health and stable energy levels.
- **Hydrate Consistently:** Even mild dehydration can intensify fatigue, irritability, and mental fog. Aiming for a gallon of water a day is a reasonable target for most adults unless otherwise advised by a medical provider.
- **Limit Sugar and Processed Foods:** Highly processed foods and sugar create blood sugar volatility, which can mimic anxiety symptoms or make them worse—especially in the late afternoon or evening

Alcohol and Drug Use: What You Need to Know

Alcohol and substances may offer short-term numbing, but they ultimately interfere with your nervous system's ability to regulate. They disrupt sleep, spike anxiety after use, and block access to the emotional clarity needed for therapy to work.

This is not about moral judgment—it's about physiology. Your brain and body cannot fully process anxiety while under the influence of substances that distort perception and inhibit regulation.

If you haven't already discussed your use of alcohol, prescription medications, or illicit substances with your therapist, now is the time. Even if your use doesn't meet criteria for addiction, it could be a hidden barrier in your healing process. Addressing it head-on allows for a more honest, strategic recovery plan.

You may be referred to an addictions specialist if needed—not because you're "failing," but because healing requires clean access to the very tools this workbook is helping you build.

Redirecting Anxious Energy

Do you ever notice that you feel so sad, unmotivated, or flat that you start to wonder if you're depressed? This might not be clinical depression—it could be what I call exhausted anxiety. When the nervous system is running on high alert for too long, it eventually burns out. The result is emotional and physical fatigue that can feel like sadness or numbness.

That's why learning to redirect anxiety's energy before you hit that wall is essential.

Anxiety symptoms—like restlessness, muscle tension, hypervigilance, or racing thoughts—are all expressions of stored energy. Left unaddressed, this energy can stagnate and lead to emotional overwhelm or shutdown. But when redirected intentionally, that same energy can be a source of motivation, creativity, and healing.

Here are ways to redirect that energy:

- **Engage in Movement:** You don't need a rigorous workout to see results. Start small—try a 10-minute walk, gentle stretching, or a short dance session. Movement discharges anxious energy and re-engages the mind-body connection.
- **Explore Creative Outlets:** Writing, painting, cooking, or playing music are excellent ways to give emotion a safe direction. Creativity provides both expression and relief, especially when words fail.
- **Try Grounding Exercises:** Grounding techniques like the 5-4-3-2-1 method, focused breathing, or using a sensory object help bring you back to the present moment, calming the nervous system and preventing energy from escalating into distress.

Redirecting anxiety doesn't mean ignoring it. It means working with it—before it wears you down.

Overcoming Barriers to Physical Activity

If starting an exercise routine feels overwhelming, you're not alone. Anxiety often convinces the brain that rest is safer than action, especially when energy is depleted. But movement—done intentionally and in small, manageable steps—is a key part of nervous system regulation.

Here's how to begin:

- **Set Realistic Goals:** Start with just 5–10 minutes of movement each day. This could be a short walk, light stretching, or simply standing and moving your arms. Consistency is more important than intensity.
- **Choose Activities You Enjoy:** Movement doesn't need to be traditional exercise. Dance, garden, hike, swim, or do yoga—anything that gets your body engaged and gives your brain a break from ruminative thoughts.
- **Find Support:** Partner with a friend, join a group class, or consider working with a coach. Support systems create accountability and make the process feel less isolating.

Tying It All Together: Barriers, Choices, and the Cost of Avoidance

By now, you've identified your barriers—those logistical, emotional, and even seemingly minor obstacles that can quietly derail progress. Some are external ("I don't have time"), others internal ("It feels too overwhelming"), and some are subtle avoidance tactics masked as responsibilities ("The cat is out of food").

But avoidance isn't neutral.

Every choice not to act—whether it's skipping therapy homework, ignoring your need for rest, or putting off physical activity—has a cost. It might be a cost to your mental clarity, physical energy, emotional resilience, or personal relationships.

This is where Cost-Benefit Analysis (CBA) comes in.

Avoidance brings short-term relief—but long-term consequences. Taking action, on the other hand, may feel uncomfortable in the moment, but it creates long-term growth, confidence, and regulation.

The next assignment will help you evaluate your current choices through this lens:
What is the short-term gain of avoidance? What is the long-term cost?
And conversely—what discomfort might come with action, but what payoff might follow?

Assignment 2: Cost-Benefit Analysis of Avoidance vs. Action

Step 1: Identify An Area of Stuckness

Consider one area where anxiety has kept you from engaging fully—this could be avoiding movement, overlooking nutrition, skipping therapeutic practices, or pulling away from meaningful connection. What part of your healing process feels stalled right now? Write it down below.

What I Avoid:

Step 2: List the Short-Term Benefits of Avoidance

Avoidance often provides immediate relief—otherwise, we wouldn't do it. What feels "easier" or "safer" when you avoid this action?

Short-Term Benefits of Avoidance:

Step 3: List the Long-Term Costs of Avoidance

What does this avoidance cost you over time? Does it impact your mental or physical health, self-confidence, or relationships?

Long-Term Costs of Avoidance:

Step 4: List the Potential Benefits of Taking Action

If you did engage in this action—even in a small way—what could change for the better?

Potential Benefits of Action:

Step 5: Weigh Your Choices

Looking at the costs and benefits, what feels more important in the long run? What small step can you take to move toward action?

What I'm Willing to Try:

Healing Is About Taking Back Control

Not in one sweeping moment, but through small, intentional choices that stack up over time. The next assignment isn't about calling yourself out for avoiding progress—it's about gaining clarity. Whether the area is therapy, movement, nutrition, or your day-to-day habits, the goal is to recognize how your patterns either support your healing—or sabotage it.

Just like the peasant in the king's test who moved the boulder and found the reward beneath it, change requires effort. The tools are in front of you. But you have to be the one to use them.

The If/Then Trap – Breaking the Cycle of Avoidance

Anxiety primes the brain to anticipate worst-case scenarios. It tries to keep you safe by analyzing every possible outcome. But this "safety" often becomes a loop of overthinking that prevents forward movement.

This shows up as **If/Then Thinking**:

- "If I go to therapy, then I'll fall apart."
- "If I try and fail, then I'll prove I'm not fixable."
- "If I trust someone, then they'll hurt me."
- "If I start now, then I'll have to admit how long I've avoided this."

This thinking *feels* like preparation, but it's avoidance disguised as logic. It keeps you mentally rehearsing pain without taking the actual step that leads to healing. And the truth is—there will always be another *then* if you let fear drive your decisions.

This next exercise helps you catch those patterns, challenge them, and reframe the "If/Then" story so it no longer runs the show.

Assignment 3: Breaking the If/Then Cycle

Step 1: Identify Your If/Then Statements

Write down at least five If/Then thoughts that have kept you stuck or hesitant to take action.

My If/Then Statements:

Step 2: Challenge the Thought

For each statement, ask yourself the following:

- Is this an absolute truth, or am I predicting the worst?
- Has this actually happened every time?
- What evidence do I have that a different outcome is possible?
- What is one small step I could take despite the anxiety?

Reframing My Statement:

Step 3: Take Action

Choose one of your reframed statements and decide on a small, concrete action you will take this week—something that challenges the belief but still feels manageable.

Action I Will Take:

Breaking Through: Moving Beyond Barriers

Barriers to healing are not dead ends—they're signals. They reveal where problem-solving, persistence, and honest self-awareness are most needed. Whether your obstacles have been external (limited time, support, or resources) or internal (fear, resistance, avoidance), the fact that you named them matters. Awareness is the first act of reclaiming control.

You've also identified how avoidance keeps you stuck. It soothes in the short term, but it steals momentum and reinforces anxiety's grip. Through the Cost-Benefit Analysis and If/Then exercise, you've begun to map the real impact of staying stagnant—and glimpsed what's possible when you take action.

What Comes Next?

- Recognize: Barriers aren't excuses. They're challenges to navigate with strategy, not shame.
- Remind Yourself: Progress doesn't require perfection. Small actions shift heavy patterns.
- Normalize Avoidance: Everyone resists discomfort. The goal is not to eliminate avoidance, but to stop letting it lead.
- Apply What You've Learned: Reframe distorted thinking. Regulate your body. Use your tools.

Healing doesn't wait for the "right time." It builds from what you do next. Each step you take—especially when it's uncomfortable—proves that change is possible. The barriers in your path were never meant to block you permanently. Like the boulder in the king's road, they exist to be moved.

COMPASSION

The Key To Long-Term Change

Compassion – The Key to Long-Term Change

Strengthening Self-Compassion

Anxiety recovery is rarely clean or linear. It's messy, exhausting, and deeply personal. There will be moments when you wonder if you're making progress or simply getting by—times when the weight of anxiety feels like too much. In these moments, self-compassion isn't optional—it's essential. Not as a soft escape, but as a stabilizing force.

Self-compassion is the practice of offering yourself the same understanding you would give a close friend—without excuses, but without harshness. It's not about denying pain or pretending things are okay. It's about meeting yourself where you are, acknowledging the difficulty, and choosing to respond with patience rather than punishment.

Why Self-Compassion Is Essential in Anxiety Recovery

Think of it like a life raft. It doesn't stop the waves of anxiety, but it keeps you from drowning in them. Self-compassion:

- **Reduces the spiral of shame and self-criticism.** Instead of "Why can't I handle this?" you can say, "This is hard, and I'm still trying."
- **Supports emotional recovery after setbacks.** Flare-ups don't have to derail everything when you meet them with grace rather than guilt.
- **Builds stamina for the long haul.** Healing isn't quick. Self-compassion gives you the emotional fuel to keep going, especially when progress is slow.

What Self-Compassion Is—And What It Isn't

Self-compassion is not about letting yourself off the hook, nor is it an excuse to stop doing the work. It doesn't mean avoiding the truth, skipping assignments, or pretending you're fine. It means creating a space where your humanity is allowed.

- It's not indulgence.
- It's not perfectionism in disguise.
- It's not weakness.

Real self-compassion requires courage—to face your pain, to name it, and to keep showing up for yourself without turning suffering into a judgment of your worth.

Tying Self-Compassion to Meaning and Purpose

Self-compassion becomes more than a practice—it becomes transformative—when it's anchored in what you value and the life you're working to rebuild. It gives shape to hard days, motivation on stuck days, and direction on uncertain days.

Defining Meaning and Purpose in Anxiety Recovery

Your Values:
What matters most to you—not what you've been told should matter, but what truly feels important? Values are the steady internal compass that guide your decisions, define your boundaries, and give shape to your healing. While material goals may come and go, your values are lasting.

Many people have never paused to truly define theirs. But especially in anxiety recovery, knowing your values isn't just a reflective exercise—it becomes a tool for direction and resilience. When you understand what you're moving toward, self-compassion no longer feels optional—it becomes necessary fuel for that journey.

You might value:

- **Connection** – cultivating meaningful relationships.
- **Freedom** – reclaiming autonomy and agency.
- **Growth** – expanding beyond old limitations.
- **Peace** – reducing inner turmoil and finding calm.
- **Contribution** – helping others or giving back.

Whatever your values are, they're yours. Naming them helps you reclaim clarity—and power.

Your Vision:
What does healing *look* like for you? This isn't about a perfect version of yourself—it's about imagining the life you want to move toward. It might be:

- Feeling confident in your ability to handle stress.
- Building secure, lasting relationships.
- Returning to activities that anxiety made you avoid.
- Speaking up without fear or overthinking.

Connecting the Dots:
How does the work you're doing—no matter how uncomfortable, slow, or invisible it feels—tie back to these values and vision?

This is where meaning comes in. It's not about dramatic moments of clarity. It's about recognizing that each time you pause to self-regulate, challenge a thought, or try again after avoidance, you're practicing alignment. The value you care about—freedom, peace, connection, growth—is being honored. And that is where transformation happens.

Assignment 4: Values Sort

This exercise will help you identify your top values—what truly matters to you on both a personal or professional level. Understanding your values is essential for your healing journey, as it helps guide decisions and actions in alignment with your core beliefs.

Step 1: Review the Values List

Below is a list of potential values. Circle your top 10 values that resonate most with you in your life right now. Don't worry about choosing "the right ones"—focus on what feels most important to you personally.

Values	Values	Values	Values
Authenticity	Balance	Belonging	Creativity
Courage	Family	Friendship	Growth
Health	Honesty	Independence	Integrity
Joy	Love	Peace	Personal Development
Purpose	Respect	Security	Spirituality
Trust	Achievement	Adventure	Altruism
Appreciation	Authentic Relationships	Beauty	Boldness

Career/Work Fulfillment	Compassion	Contribution	Consistency
Contentment	Curiosity	Determination	Diversity
Empowerment	Equality	Expressiveness	Fairness
Faith	Flexibility	Forgiveness	Generosity
Gratitude	Growth/Progress	Happiness	Harmony
Healing	Helpfulness	Innovation	Insight
Knowledge	Leadership	Love & Affection	Openness
Peace of Mind	Patience	Persistence	Purposefulness
Respect for Others	Responsibility	Self-Acceptance	Self-Worth
Service	Simplicity	Spontaneity	Strength
Support	Teamwork	Wisdom	Zest

Step 2: Narrow it Down

From your list of 10 values, **choose your top 5**. Write them down in the table below.

Top 5 Personal Values	My Definition & Meaning
1.	
2.	
3.	
4.	
5.	

Step 3: Define Your Top 2 Values

From your top 5 values, select two that hold the utmost importance to you. In 10 words or less, write your personal definition of each value.

Most Important Values	My Definition & Meaning
1.	
2.	

Step 4: Reflect on How These Values Show Up in Your Life

Now that you've defined your values, think about how they play a role in your everyday life. Consider how your values influence the way you react to situations, make decisions, and communicate with others.

- **Question 1:** How do you see these values being used in how you react, make decisions, and communicate?
- **Question 2:** In what ways do you see these values helping you navigate anxiety recovery and your healing journey?

Note: The Importance of Self-Compassion

You may be tempted to skim this section or write it off as "too soft" or unnecessary. If you're someone who's used to pushing through with grit, discipline, and a "get over it" mindset, this part might feel foreign—maybe even irritating. That's valid. But ask yourself honestly:

Has the way you've treated yourself up until now helped you heal?
Has relentless self-criticism made you feel safer, more capable, or more resilient?

If the answer is no, then it's time to consider a different approach.

Self-compassion isn't sugary or passive. It's a deliberate shift away from the voice that says, *"You're not doing enough,"* toward one that says, *"You're doing the hard work, and you're still standing."* It's not about blind positivity—it's about honest kindness. It's about giving yourself the same grace you'd offer someone else who's hurting.

This is a critical step in anxiety recovery because when the inner critic runs the show, healing stalls. By practicing self-compassion, you give yourself the room to make mistakes, face setbacks, and still continue forward—not out of force, but out of grounded strength.

If the old way hasn't worked, this might be the shift you need.

Assignment 5: Cultivating Self-Compassion and Purpose in Anxiety Recovery

Step 1: Recognize Where You Struggle with Self-Compassion
Take time to reflect on how you treat yourself when anxiety symptoms arise.

- When was the last time you criticized yourself for how you're managing your recovery?
- What did you say to yourself?
- How might you respond differently next time?
  Write your thoughts:

Step 2: Define Your Why
Ask yourself: Why am I doing this work? What kind of life do I want to create, and how does working through anxiety fit into that vision? *(Pull from your values)*

Write down your answers:

Step 3: Take Action—Compassion in Practice

Self-compassion is not just about what you think; it's about what you do. Small, intentional actions remind you: *I am worth the effort.*

- What does this look like for you? It could be taking a mindful walk, writing in a journal, meditating, or simply allowing yourself a quiet moment to breathe. These acts are not indulgences—they are vital reminders of your worth.

  Write down your act of compassion:

The Reality of Anxiety Recovery

Recovery from anxiety isn't a straight path, easy, or perfect. It requires patience, persistence, and a willingness to face discomfort—often repeatedly. There will be days when the weight of your anxiety feels unbearable and progress feels out of reach. That doesn't mean you've failed. It means you're in the middle of the process.

Healing isn't about arriving at some flawless version of yourself. It's about showing up—in small, consistent ways that add up over time. It's brushing your teeth when you don't want to, taking a walk when your body says freeze, or doing a CBT exercise even though you're exhausted. These actions matter.

Self-compassion isn't fluff—it's fuel. It gives you the ability to keep going without adding the weight of judgment to what you're already carrying. It's a discipline that allows space for both effort and imperfection. Real recovery is built on acknowledging where you are, refusing to let avoidance take over, and choosing to keep going—even if it's messy.

The Power of Recovery: A Testament to Healing

Anxiety, in its healthiest form, serves a purpose. It's the brain's early warning system—a signal that says, *"Something might need your attention."* Think of it like the boiling pot on the stove. A low simmer keeps you alert, focused, and motivated. It can push you to meet a deadline, prepare for a tough conversation, or avoid a dangerous situation. That's anxiety doing its job.

But when the pot boils over—when anxiety becomes constant, overwhelming, or misdirected—it stops serving you and starts controlling you. That's the type of anxiety this workbook addresses. The kind that narrows your world, disrupts your body, hijacks your thoughts, and keeps you in survival mode long after the threat is gone.

Recovery doesn't mean getting rid of anxiety completely. It means regulating the flame under the pot. It means learning how to listen to anxiety without letting it run your life. It means distinguishing between real threats and imagined ones, between useful discomfort and unnecessary suffering.

I've seen this transformation happen. One client, whose anxiety began in early childhood, believed for decades that she was permanently broken. Together, we worked through what you're doing now—reframing distorted thoughts, regulating her nervous system, confronting the patterns that kept her stuck. It was hard. She didn't always believe in the process. But she did the work.

By the end of our time together, the same assessments that once measured high clinical anxiety showed something else: Stability. Clarity. Function. Life was no longer shaped by what she feared, but by what she valued. The pot was still on the stove—but the heat was manageable.

That's what recovery looks like. Not perfection. Not a life without stress. But a life where *you* are the one in control of the dial.

Why Self-Compassion Feels Unnatural—And Why You Need It

If you're rolling your eyes at the idea of self-compassion, good. That probably means this section is especially for you.

If you've been taught that "pushing through" is strength, or if you've lived most of your life numbing out rather than naming what's going on inside, then compassion might feel foreign—or like weakness. It isn't.

Here's what you need to know:

Anxiety physically rewires your brain. It trains your nervous system to expect danger, interpret discomfort as threat, and stay stuck in hypervigilance. In that state, self-compassion isn't just unfamiliar—it feels unsafe.

But this is where the work begins.

Self-compassion isn't about ignoring the problem or pretending everything is okay. It's about stepping outside of the loop of criticism and shame. It's about teaching your brain to relate to pain differently.

Every time you stop and acknowledge your struggle without judgment…
Every time you respond to your anxiety with steadiness instead of fear…
Every time you practice compassionate reflection instead of self-blame…

…you're changing the wiring. You're building emotional flexibility and resilience.

This isn't soft. It's neuroscience. It's cognitive re-patterning. It's rewiring your brain to support recovery, not sabotage it.

Assignment 6: Letter to Myself – Cultivating Self-Compassion

Purpose: Anxiety has a way of distorting how you view yourself—convincing you that you're weak, broken, or failing because you feel overwhelmed. It often leaves people extending compassion to everyone but themselves. This exercise is designed to help shift that internal dialogue.

By writing a compassionate letter to yourself, you'll begin practicing a different voice—one rooted in truth, patience, and emotional regulation. You are not writing to "fix" anything. You are writing to acknowledge that navigating anxiety is hard—and to remind yourself that you are doing the best you can.

Instructions:

1. **Imagine a person you care about—someone who struggles with anxiety just like you.** What would you say to them if they told you they felt overwhelmed, hopeless, or exhausted? Would you criticize them, or would you comfort them?
2. **Now, write that letter to yourself.** Use that same compassion and understanding—but direct it inward. You don't have to force yourself to believe things that feel fake or sugary. Just write from a place of honesty, support, and respect for how hard this work can be.

In your letter, aim to include:

- **Validation:** Acknowledge what you've been through and how anxiety has affected you. Recognize that anxiety symptoms are not a personal failure—they're a sign your nervous system has been overworked and overstimulated.
- **Encouragement:** Speak to yourself with the same steady, supportive tone you'd use with someone else. You don't need cheerleading—you need grounding truth and perspective.
- **Commitment:** End your letter with one small promise. This could be a promise to rest, to try again, or simply to stop being so hard on yourself when things get tough.

Example Letter Opening:

Dear [Your Name],

I know anxiety has taken so much from you—your energy, your sleep, your sense of safety. I also know how hard you've worked to face it. You've shown up for yourself in ways that no one else can fully understand, and even if progress feels slow, you are making it.

You don't have to earn rest. You don't have to prove your worth through perfection. And you don't have to keep carrying the weight of every anxious thought as if it's the truth.

You are not your anxiety. You are not weak. You are learning how to live differently—and that's one of the bravest things anyone can do.

With respect and care,
[Your Name]

DEAR SELF,
LET'S TRY THIS COMPASSION THING-

Therapist Check In

Activity	Date Completed	Client Initials	Therapist Initials
A1. Naming Your Barriers			
A2. Cost-Benefit Analysis of Avoidance			
A3. Breaking the If/Then Cycle			
A4. Values Sort			
A5. Cultivating Self-Compassion and Purpose in Anxiety Recovery			
A6. Letter to Myself – Cultivating Self-Compassion			

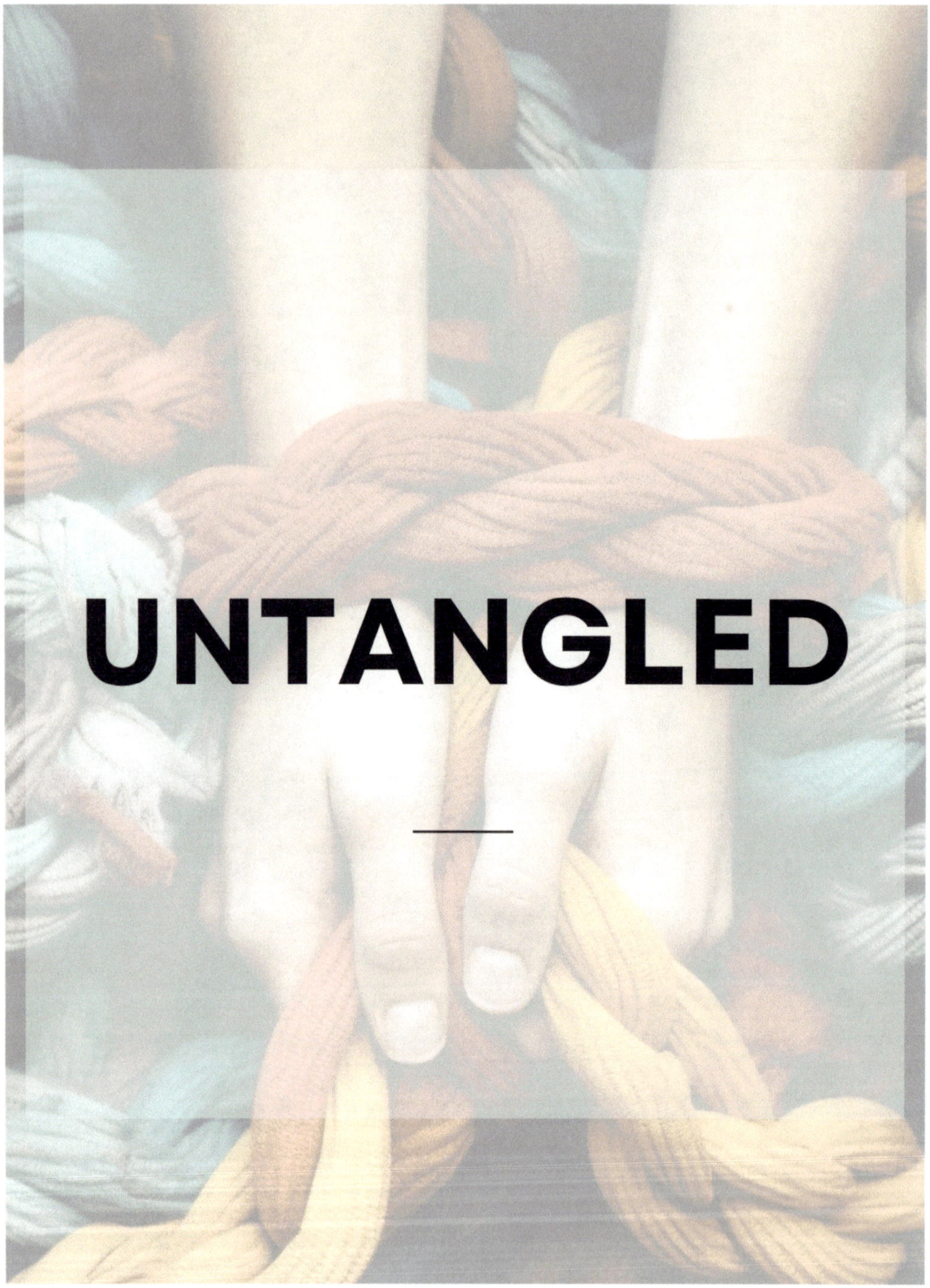
UNTANGLED

Untangling Anxiety: Your Next Steps Forward

Reaching this point in the guide is no small feat. Throughout these chapters, you've faced anxiety with honesty and courage—exploring how it shows up in your body, how attachment patterns shape your responses, and how tools like behavioral experiments, cognitive reframing, and nervous system regulation can support lasting change.

This guide reflects my broader mission: to redefine counseling as direct, compassionate, and grounded in science. By blending evidence-based strategies with empathy and a deep understanding of the human experience, I aim to provide tools that drive meaningful and lasting change.

As you move forward, remember this: you don't need to eliminate anxiety to heal—you need to change your relationship with it. Every small step you take—confronting a trigger, practicing self-compassion, or reconnecting with purpose—strengthens the foundation for your future.

There may be days when you feel stuck, exhausted, or unsure of your progress. That's normal. With deliberate action, self-reflection, and the willingness to keep moving forward, you can build a life that is no longer defined by anxiety but by resilience, meaning, and possibility.

So—what now?

- **Use the tools that work for you.** You don't have to use everything in this workbook—just what helps.
- **Stay consistent.** Progress isn't about doing it perfectly; it's about doing it regularly.
  Know your patterns. Expect resistance, avoidance, and doubt. Use what you've learned to navigate through, not around them.
- **Reach out when needed.** Healing doesn't mean going it alone. Support is strength.
- **Celebrate the small wins.** Every time you show up differently, you're changing your brain—and your story.

TOOLS & RESOURCES

Tools & Resources

The following pages offer additional tools and resources to support your healing journey as you move beyond this workbook. It's important to remember that anxiety recovery is not a straightforward or predictable path. Progress can look different each day, and having structured ways to reflect, track, and continue growing is essential. The Anxiety Recovery Progress Tracker, journaling pages, and self-reflection prompts are here for you to revisit whenever needed, providing a space to document insights and emotional processing.

These tools are meant to be used during and between therapy sessions—whether to note important reflections, track your progress, or record any new exercises introduced in therapy. While this workbook offers a structured framework, therapy itself is a dynamic process. You will be introduced to new skills, personalized strategies, and interventions that may not be covered here. Rather than overwhelming you with an exhaustive workbook, this section is designed with flexibility in mind—giving you a space to focus on what matters most for your unique healing journey.

Use these pages in whatever way feels most meaningful to you, remembering that healing is an active, evolving process that requires ongoing attention and adaptation.

Anxiety Recovery Progress Tracker

Use this tracker to monitor your progress as you work through the guide. For each section, document your reflections, completed exercises, and any insights or breakthroughs. This tool will help you stay consistent and see how far you've come in your recovery journey.

How to Use This Tracker

- **Be Honest:** This isn't about achieving perfection—it's about recognizing patterns and staying intentional.
- **Reflect Often:** Review your notes regularly to identify growth and areas needing additional focus.
- **Celebrate Wins:** Acknowledge every step forward, no matter how small.

This tracker is your companion on the journey forward. It is a place to record your work and remind yourself of your progress. Keep it nearby and use it as often as you need to stay grounded and focused.

Anxiety Recovery Progress Tracker

Key Exercise or Reflection	Date Complete	Your Insights or Breakthroughs
Nervous System Regulation		
Understanding Attachment		
Cognitive Tools		
Behavioral Exercises		
Overcoming Barriers		
Strengthening Self-Compassion		
Meaning-Making Activities		
Daily Progress Check		

Key Exercise or Reflection	Date Complete	Your Insights or Breakthroughs

Regulation Exercises

The following exercises, along with the tools you've learned through therapy—such as your Calm Plan and various regulation techniques—are all resources you can use to help regulate your nervous system, manage emotional distress, and restore balance in both your body and mind. These tools are designed to empower you to navigate challenging emotions, regain control, and create a sense of calm. As you continue on your healing journey, these techniques will become invaluable assets for maintaining resilience and emotional well-being.

Progressive Muscle Relaxation (PMR)

Instructions:

1. **Find a Comfortable Position**
   Sit or lie down in a comfortable position. Close your eyes and take a few deep breaths.

2. **Take Deep Breaths**
   Inhale deeply through your nose, hold for a moment, and exhale through your mouth.

3. **Start with Your Hands and Forearms**

   - **Tense:** Curl your fingers into a fist and tighten your hand and forearm muscles. Hold for 5-10 seconds.
   - **Release:** Slowly release and focus on the relaxation.

4. **Move to Your Upper Arms and Biceps**

   - **Tense:** Tighten your biceps by bending your arms at the elbows. Hold for 5-10 seconds.
   - **Release:** Relax your arms and notice the release.

5. **Relax Your Shoulders**

   - **Tense:** Lift your shoulders toward your ears. Hold for 5-10 seconds.
   - **Release:** Lower your shoulders and relax.

6. **Tense Your Neck Muscles**

   - **Tense:** Gently press your head backward. Hold for 5-10 seconds.
   - **Release:** Relax your neck.

7. **Focus on Your Face**

   - **Tense:** Tighten the muscles in your face (scrunch forehead, clench jaw). Hold for 5-10 seconds.
   - **Release:** Relax your face and jaw.

8. **Move to Your Chest and Stomach**

    - **Tense:** Tighten the muscles in your chest and stomach. Hold for 5-10 seconds.
    - **Release:** Exhale and relax these areas.

9. **Tense Your Legs (Quadriceps)**

    - **Tense:** Tighten the muscles in your thighs. Hold for 5-10 seconds.
    - **Release:** Relax your legs.

10. **Relax Your Feet and Toes**

    - **Tense:** Curl your toes downward. Hold for 5-10 seconds.
    - **Release:** Relax your feet and toes.

11. **Final Relaxation**
    Take a moment to breathe deeply and notice the calm throughout your entire body.

Autogenic Training (AT)

Using self-guided verbal cues to create sensations of warmth, heaviness, and calm. See *Somatic Awareness* section.

Box Breathing (4-4-4-4)

Inhale for 4 seconds, hold for 4, exhale for 4, and hold for 4.

Diaphragmatic Breathing: Diaphragmatic breathing, also known as deep belly breathing, focuses on fully engaging the diaphragm, rather than shallow breathing from the chest. This technique is essential for activating the parasympathetic nervous system, which is responsible for the body's relaxation response. By breathing deeply into the belly, you signal to your body that it is time to calm down, reducing stress and promoting a sense of relaxation. This type of breathing helps to counteract the effects of the stress response, bringing your heart rate down and allowing your mind and body to feel more grounded.

4-7-8 Breathing: Inhale for 4 seconds, hold for 7, and exhale for 8.

Cold Water Immersion or Temperature Shifting

Using cold water immersion or applying cold to areas like your wrists, face, or chest can be an incredibly effective way to activate the vagus nerve and reduce distress. You can achieve this through a cold plunge, facing a cold shower, or even squeezing ice cubes in your hands. This technique helps shock your system out of the fight-or-flight response, which is driven by the sympathetic nervous system. When your body is in fight-or-flight, it is flooded with stress hormones that heighten your sense of anxiety, fear, and urgency.

Cold exposure immediately triggers a physiological response that helps shift your body into a state of calm by stimulating the vagus nerve, which is part of the parasympathetic nervous system—responsible for rest and relaxation. This activation helps slow your heart rate, lower blood pressure, and calm the body's overactive stress response.

Once your body is soothed, you are better able to engage in cognitive reframing. This means that, with the physical distress lowered, your mind has a better chance to rationalize and challenge any distressing or irrational thoughts. Essentially, cold water immersion is a quick reset that allows you to shift from emotional turmoil to a state where new, healthier perspectives can take hold.

Bilateral Stimulation & Tapping

Why It Works:
Bilateral stimulation, including tapping exercises like butterfly tapping and leg tapping, is effective for reducing stress and calming the nervous system. These techniques involve alternating left and right side stimulation, which helps engage both hemispheres of the brain. This bilateral movement has been shown to promote hemispheric integration, a process that enhances communication between the two sides of the brain, leading to greater emotional regulation and calmness. This process helps break the cycle of emotional overwhelm, allowing you to better process and regulate difficult emotions.

Butterfly Tapping:
To perform butterfly tapping, cross your arms over your chest with your hands resting under your collar bone. Alternate tapping each side gently in a rhythm that feels comfortable, slowly. This rhythmic bilateral stimulation creates a calming effect on the brain and body, helping to regulate the stress response. Butterfly tapping can activate the parasympathetic nervous system, which promotes relaxation. It's particularly helpful in moments of high stress or when emotional overwhelm is present, as it helps shift the brain into a more grounded, calm state.

Leg Tapping:
For leg tapping, sit comfortably and alternate gentle taps on each thigh. The alternating tapping creates a soothing, rhythmic movement that helps calm the body and mind. This technique is an effective way to ground yourself, reduce physical tension, and induce a sense of relaxation.

Grounding Techniques

5-4-3-2-1 Method:

The 5-4-3-2-1 Method is a grounding technique designed to help you reconnect to the present moment, especially during times of emotional overwhelm or anxiety. This exercise engages your senses and helps bring you back to the here and now, reducing feelings of dissociation or panic.

- **5 things you see**: Take a look around your environment and identify five things you can see. Focus on details like shapes, colors, or textures.
- **4 things you can touch**: Pay attention to four things you can physically feel—whether it's the texture of the chair you're sitting on, the sensation of your clothes against your skin, or the feel of the ground beneath you.
- **3 things you hear**: Focus on three sounds in your environment. These could be distant noises, like birds chirping or the hum of traffic, or closer sounds, like your breathing or the rustling of fabric.
- **2 things you can smell**: Notice two distinct smells around you. If there's nothing around to smell, take a deep breath and bring your attention to your own scent or any fragrance in the air.
- **1 thing you can taste**: Focus on one thing you can taste. It could be the aftertaste of your last meal, a sip of water, or the air on your tongue.

This method helps distract the mind from distressing thoughts, creating a present-centered awareness that brings you back to a sense of control and calm. It also provides a mental reset by engaging the senses and calming the nervous system.

Feet on the Floor Technique:

The Feet on the Floor Technique is a simple yet effective grounding practice to help you feel more stable and centered. To do this, sit in a comfortable chair with your feet flat on the floor. Focus on the sensation of your feet pressing into the ground, feeling the stability of the earth beneath you. As you focus on this grounded feeling, imagine that your feet are rooted into the ground, just like the base of a tree. This practice encourages physical awareness, helping you feel anchored in the present moment and connected to the earth.

This technique is great for when you need a quick reset to regain focus or calm your nervous system. By shifting your attention to the physical sensation of your feet on the floor, you disrupt unhelpful thought patterns and bring your mind back to your body, promoting a sense of balance and control.

Sensory Regulation

Engaging the senses is a powerful tool for calming the body and mind, especially when you feel overwhelmed or disconnected. Sensory regulation involves using different sensory stimuli—such as aromatherapy, textured objects, soothing sounds, or warmth—to promote relaxation and restore balance in the nervous system. These techniques can help shift your body from a heightened state of stress to a more relaxed and centered one.

- **Aromatherapy**: Essential oils like lavender, chamomile, or eucalyptus can have a calming effect on the mind and body. Using a diffuser, applying a few drops to your skin (mixed with a carrier oil), or simply inhaling the scent can help lower stress levels and promote emotional balance.

- **Textured Objects**: Holding or touching objects with different textures can be soothing. Examples include a soft fabric, a stress ball, or even a textured stone. The tactile experience of feeling different surfaces can help ground you and redirect your focus from overwhelming thoughts to physical sensations.

- **Soothing Sounds**: Listening to calming music, nature sounds (like ocean waves or rainfall), or white noise can help reduce anxiety and create a peaceful environment. These sounds can activate the parasympathetic nervous system, which is responsible for relaxation.

- **Warmth**: The sensation of warmth—whether from a heated blanket, warm cup of tea, or a hot shower—can help relax the muscles and calm the body. It encourages a feeling of safety and comfort, making it easier to settle into a state of calm.

By engaging one or more of these sensory experiences, you provide your body with a sense of calm and stability. Sensory regulation can be an effective tool to help manage stress and bring you back into the present moment.

Self-Holding Exercises

Self-holding exercises involve applying gentle pressure to yourself in ways that promote a sense of comfort, safety, and emotional regulation. These exercises are particularly helpful when you need to reconnect with your body and soothe yourself during moments of distress. By gently holding or touching parts of your body, you activate a calming response that helps ease tension and reduce anxiety.

Techniques:

- **Hugging Yourself:** Cross your arms over your chest and gently hug yourself. Squeeze lightly and feel the comfort of your embrace. This action provides a sense of emotional security and physical closeness, which can help regulate the nervous system and calm overwhelming feelings.

- **Placing Hands on Your Heart or Stomach:** Gently place one or both hands on your heart or stomach. Feel the rise and fall of your breath as you tune into the physical sensation of your body. This exercise can help create a grounding effect, reducing the intensity of emotions and helping you focus on the present moment.

- **Weighted Blanket:** Using a weighted blanket can provide gentle, even pressure on your body, which mimics the sensation of being held. This pressure is soothing and helps activate the body's parasympathetic nervous system, promoting relaxation and emotional stability.

- **Compression Clothing:** Compression garments or clothing, such as weighted vests or compression shirts, can offer a sense of physical grounding and help reduce feelings of anxiety or stress. The pressure they provide is calming and creates a feeling of being supported.

These self-holding exercises and tools are simple yet effective methods for increasing self-compassion and establishing a feeling of safety. By gently applying pressure to key areas of your body or using supportive materials like weighted blankets and compression clothing, you can activate your body's natural relaxation response, helping to ease distress and encourage emotional self-regulation.

Visualization & Mental Rehearsal

Visualization is a powerful technique that allows you to mentally escape from stress or anxiety by imagining a safe, peaceful place. By creating a mental image of a calming environment, you can shift your nervous system from the fight-or-flight response into a state of relaxation. This process helps reduce emotional intensity and encourages the body and mind to experience calmness and safety, even in the midst of stress.

How It Works:

- **Create Your Safe Place:** Close your eyes and take a few deep breaths. Imagine a place where you feel completely safe, peaceful, and at ease. It could be a beach, a quiet forest, a room with soft lighting, or anywhere that feels relaxing to you.

- **Engage All Your Senses:** To make the visualization more vivid, try to engage all five of your senses. Imagine the sounds you hear in this place, the smells, the textures, and the sights around you. The more details you can add, the more real the experience will feel.

- **Feel the Calm:** As you visualize this safe place, focus on the feeling of peace and comfort. Let your body relax as you imagine yourself fully immersed in this calming environment. Notice how your breathing slows down, and your muscles soften.

Mental Rehearsal:
Visualization can also be used as a form of mental rehearsal for situations you find challenging. Imagine yourself handling a stressful event with calm and confidence. By mentally rehearsing these situations, you can reduce anxiety and build resilience, allowing your mind and body to feel more prepared for real-life challenges.

Thought Stopping

Thought stopping is a technique that can help you interrupt distressing or negative thoughts before they escalate or spiral out of control. While not specifically a regulation tool, it serves as an effective way to regain control over your thought process and prevent overwhelming emotions from taking over.

How It Works:

- **Interrupt Negative Thoughts:** When you notice a negative or distressing thought, immediately say "Stop" out loud or visualize a stop sign. This breaks the automatic flow of the thought, helping to disrupt its power and intensity.

- **Pair with a Physical Action:** To further reinforce the interruption, pair the "Stop" with a physical action such as clapping your hands, snapping your fingers, or even gently tapping your body. This movement engages your body and interrupts the current neural network associated with that thought, helping to create a new, healthier pathway for thought processes.

- **Re-focus:** After interrupting the thought, consciously redirect your focus to something more neutral or calming. You can focus on your breath, engage in a grounding technique, or think about a positive memory or image.

Thought stopping acts as a cognitive interruption—it doesn't necessarily change the content of the thought immediately, but it helps you regain control and prevent further rumination. By practicing this technique, you can become more aware of your thought patterns and stop distressing thoughts before they overwhelm you.

What Works for You?

Beyond the exercises and techniques outlined in this workbook, you may already have other tools and strategies that help you effectively regulate your emotions. It's important to recognize that everyone has their own unique methods of coping and finding balance. These could include practices you've developed over time or ones that you've found helpful through previous experiences or other resources. Remember, the journey of healing is personal, and the strategies that resonate most with you are the ones that will be most effective.

In addition to the exercises provided, feel free to explore further tools and resources. You can visit www.untangledmind.net/vagal for more information on vagal regulation techniques and other helpful materials.

Take a moment to reflect on what has worked for you in the past or what feels like it might be helpful as you continue your journey. Write down any additional strategies, methods, or practices that help you feel more grounded and balanced on the following page.

By documenting these strategies, you create a personal toolkit to draw upon when you need it most.

REGULATION TOOLBOX

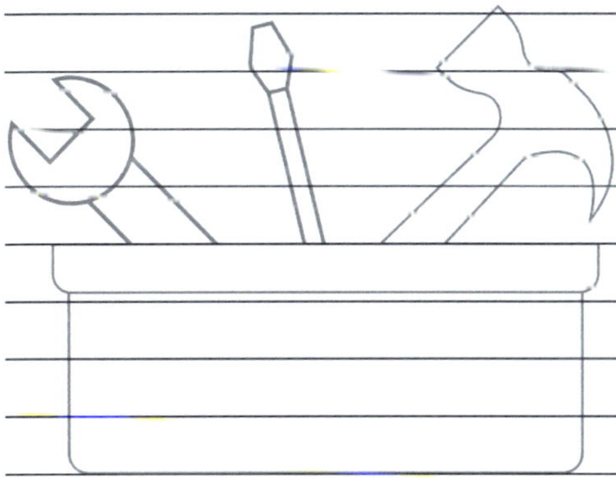

25 Journaling Prompts for Anxiety Healing and Growth

1. When anxiety shows up, what is the first thing I tend to do? Does that response help or hurt in the long term?
2. What specific thoughts or situations tend to make my anxiety spiral? Can I identify a pattern?
3. What does "being in control" mean to me, and how does anxiety distort that need?
4. When I avoid something out of fear, what is the cost to me mentally, emotionally, or physically?
5. What assumptions do I make about worst-case scenarios, and how often do they actually happen?
6. How do I know the difference between my anxious thoughts and my rational thoughts?
7. What bodily sensations do I most associate with anxiety, and how can I respond to them with curiosity rather than panic?
8. What do I believe people will think of me if I appear anxious, and where did that belief come from?
9. If I stop trying to manage everyone's perception of me, what would that free up for me emotionally?
10. What does certainty mean to me, and how does my search for it increase my anxiety?
11. How do I respond when plans change suddenly? What does that reveal about my internal sense of safety?
12. What small decisions feel overwhelming to me, and what beliefs are making them feel so high-stakes?
13. What are three thoughts I repeat to myself when I feel anxious, and how can I reframe each one more realistically?
14. What coping behaviors do I rely on that offer short-term relief but cause long-term distress?
15. What would it look like to respond to anxious thoughts without immediately trying to "fix" or suppress them?
16. When I catastrophize, what am I trying to prepare for or protect myself from?
17. What does emotional safety look like in a relationship, and how do I respond when it's not there?
18. What rules do I live by that anxiety created—but that no longer serve me?
19. How do I know when I'm ruminating vs. reflecting? What shifts the line between the two?
20. What is one anxious narrative I've told myself for years—and what's the evidence that challenges it?
21. If I believed I was capable of handling discomfort, how might that change my behavior?
22. When I feel anxious, what part of me is asking for attention? What do I usually ignore in those moments?
23. What is one decision I've been avoiding due to fear of making the wrong choice? What's the cost of continuing to avoid it?
24. How does my anxiety affect the people around me? What would change if I allowed more honesty in those relationships?
25. What would it mean for me to stop waiting for anxiety to disappear and start building a life around resilience instead?

Distress Thermometer

100 Highest Distress. Crisis.

90 Extreme Distress

80 High Distress

70 Strong Distress. Focus Impaired

60 Strong to Moderate Distress

50 Moderate Distress

40 Moderate to Mild Distress

30 Mild Distress No Functioning Issues

20 Minimal Distress

10 Alert Focused. Concentrating

0/100 Relaxed Calm . Possible Freeze

Assessment Results Tracker

This page is designed to help you track your results from the assessments you will complete throughout your healing journey. For each assessment, you will have space to summarize key insights, reflect on how the results make you feel, and set goals for moving forward. Over time, this will give you a comprehensive view of your progress.

Instructions:

- For each assessment, fill out the relevant section below.
- Use this tracker throughout your healing process to note any shifts in your thoughts, behaviors, and emotional responses.

Assessment Results Tracker

Assessment	Date Completed	Summary of Results

Reflection Assessment:

Emotional Response:

- How did you feel about the results?

Strengths:

- Identify any strengths that were highlighted.

Areas for Growth:

- What area(s) need further attention or exploration?

Action Steps/Goals:

- What specific actions will you take based on this assessment's results?

Reflection Assessment:

Emotional Response:

- How did you feel about the results?

Strengths:

- Identify any strengths that were highlighted.

Areas for Growth:

- What area(s) need further attention or exploration?

Action Steps/Goals:

- What specific actions will you take based on this assessment's results?

Reflection Assessment:

Emotional Response:

- How did you feel about the results?

Strengths:

- Identify any strengths that were highlighted.

Areas for Growth:

- What area(s) need further attention or exploration?

Action Steps/Goals:

- What specific actions will you take based on this assessment's results?

Emotions Wheel

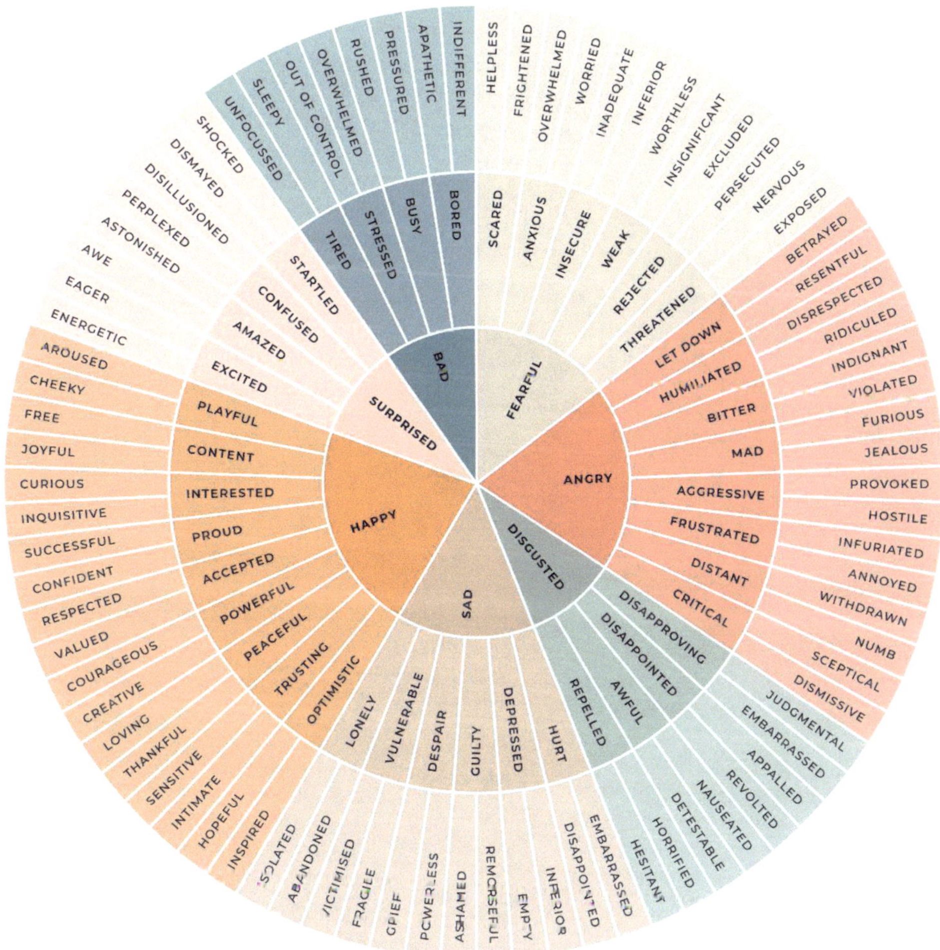

Notes

Healing is filled with insights, challenges, and personal breakthroughs that don't always fit neatly into structured exercises. This section is yours. Whether you use it to process thoughts, jot down additional assignments from our sessions, or reflect on moments of growth, let this be a space where your healing unfolds freely.

Notes

Notes

Notes

Notes

Notes

WRAP UP

Wrap Up

Acknowledgments

This workbook exists because of the people who have shaped, challenged, and supported me throughout my journey as a clinician.

To my clients—your courage, honesty, and determination are the reason I do this work. Your resilience continues to move me and deepen my commitment to this mission.

To my husband—your love, laughter, and unwavering belief in me have carried me through the hardest seasons. You are my steady place, and I'm endlessly grateful for you.

To my sons—thank you for seeing strength in me even when I felt threadbare. Your encouragement has been a quiet force behind every page of this guide.

To my family and friends—thank you for your steady support throughout the years—through every chapter of my life as an entrepreneur, mother, friend, and therapist. And to all the therapists who have poured into me along the way, thank you for your teaching, wisdom, and care.

And above all, to God—this work, this mission, and every step of this journey are Yours. I pray it all brings You glory and help others find freedom, healing, and clarity.

About the Author

Piper Harris, MA, APC, NPT-C, is a trauma-informed therapist and the founder of Untangled Mind, LLC based in the suburbs of Atlanta, GA. With over two decades of experience in mental health and behavioral coaching, Piper specializes in anxiety, trauma, and grief counseling through a data-driven, neuropsychotherapy-informed approach.

Piper holds a Master of Arts in Clinical Mental Health Counseling from Liberty University. She is certified in TEAM-CBT (Level 1) and Neuropsychotherapy (NPT-C) and is currently completing EMDR training. She integrates Third Wave CBT and attachment-based therapy, ensuring clients experience measurable progress and real transformation.

Beyond individual therapy, Piper is a speaker, author, and advocate for ethical, results-based mental health care. She has worked in hospital psychiatric units, private practice, coaching, and leadership development, providing a multidimensional approach to mental wellness.

When not working with clients, Piper enjoys deepening her neuroscience knowledge, engaging in her faith, and spending time with her family and friends.

Learn more about her work at:
www.untangledmind.net
LinkedIn: linkedin.com/in/untangledmindllc/

Further Reading

The following books and resources have influenced my approach to anxiety, healing, and emotional regulation. While they were not directly cited in this workbook, they provide valuable insights and support.

Originality and Acknowledgment

While the work presented in this book is original, it is important to acknowledge that my approach has been deeply influenced by years of training, research, and the work of many scholars and practitioners in the field of anxiety, trauma, therapy, and emotional regulation. All concepts, techniques, and frameworks used are presented with the utmost respect for the work of others, and no material within this workbook has been intentionally plagiarized. The goal is to offer a blend of evidence-based practices and personal insights to help guide you through your healing journey.

- Beck, A. T. (1976). *Cognitive Therapy and the Emotional Disorders.* International Universities Press.
- Bowlby, J. (1988). *A Secure Base: Parent-Child Attachment and Healthy Human Development.* Basic Books.
- Brackett, M. (2019). *Permission to Feel: Unlocking the Power of Emotions to Help Our Kids, Ourselves, and Our Society Thrive.* Celadon Books.
- Burns, D. D. (2020). *Feeling Great: The Revolutionary New Treatment for Depression and Anxiety.* HarperOne.
- Cozolino, L. (2017). *The Neuroscience of Psychotherapy: Healing the Social Brain* (3rd ed.). W. W. Norton & Company.
- Porges, S. W. (2011). *The Polyvagal Theory: Neurophysiological Foundations of Emotions, Attachment, Communication, and Self-Regulation.* W. W. Norton & Company.
- Siegel, D. J. (2012). *The Developing Mind: How Relationships and the Brain Interact to Shape Who We Are.* Guilford Press.
- Shrier, A. (2023). *Bad Therapy: Why the Mental Health Industry is Failing Us.* Sentinel.
- Sweeton, J. (n.d.). *Neuropsychotherapy for clinicians*. Online CE Credits. https://onlinececredits.com/courses/neuropsychotherapy-for-clinicians/
- Türk, F. (2024). *anxietytic Stress and Post-anxietytic Growth in Individuals Who Have Had Covid-19: The Mediating Effect of Resilience and Moderating Effect of Psychological Flexibility.*

Closing Thoughts

Anxiety can be a mess and overcoming it can be difficult. It's a process that requires time, intention, and the willingness to confront what feels overwhelming. This workbook has offered practical, evidence-based tools to help you regulate your nervous system, reframe anxious thoughts, and move through life with greater clarity and resilience.

But true transformation doesn't happen in isolation. The most powerful growth often comes when we pair knowledge with connection—whether through therapy, community, faith, or continued reflection. Your work here matters. Every section completed, every insight gained, and every barrier faced is part of a larger shift in how you relate to your anxiety—and to yourself.

This may be the beginning of your healing or one step along the way. Either way, remember: progress isn't measured by perfection. It's found in the consistent choice to show up, keep going, and believe that something different is possible.

You are not alone. Keep moving forward.

> *"Do you wish to be great? Then begin by being. Do you desire to construct a vast and lofty fabric? Think first about the foundations of humility."*
>
> *— St. Augustine*

Where to Go from Here

Are you looking for additional support, exercises, or guidance? Visit **www.untangledmind.net** for free resources, blog posts, scheduling of counseling services for Georgia residents, and upcoming programs.

Made in the USA
Columbia, SC
18 August 2025

61473054R00135